Google Script: Enterprise Application Essentials

James Ferreira

Beijing · Cambridge · Farnham · Köln · Sebastopol · Tokyo

Google Script: Enterprise Application Essentials
by James Ferreira

Published by O'Reilly Media, Inc., 1005 Gravenstein Highway North, Sebastopol, CA 95472.

O'Reilly books may be purchased for educational, business, or sales promotional use. Online editions are also available for most titles (*http://my.safaribooksonline.com*). For more information, contact our corporate/institutional sales department: (800) 998-9938 or *corporate@oreilly.com*.

Editor: Mary Treseler	**Cover Designer:** Karen Montgomery
Production Editor: Melanie Yarbrough	**Interior Designer:** David Futato
	Illustrator: Robert Romano

Revision History for the First Edition:
    2012-01-13   First release
See *http://oreilly.com/catalog/errata.csp?isbn=9781449318529* for release details.

ISBN: 978-1-449-31852-9

[LSI]

1327087133

Table of Contents

Part III.   UI Element Examples

Preface

Introduction

If you are reading this book, there is a good chance you have heard of Google and its powerful office productivity suite, Google Apps. Google offers search, email, word processing, and hundreds of other cloud applications and services that can be available to the individual and can scale all the way up to massive corporations and governments. As one of Google's most popular services, Google Apps offers some of the best online office products available and is an excellent example of web-based applications that out perform legacy desktop software.

This book is about Google Apps Script, which is a service that runs from Google Apps, like Sites and Documents. Google Script is extremely powerful when automating many of the tasks required by day-to-day spreadsheet operations, but it also scales up to provide a complete application platform. If you are coming from a Microsoft Office direction, you can think of it as the macros for Google Documents, but unlike simple macros in MS Office, Google Script has a mature online editor with all the features one would expect in a development platform. Unleash Google Script's user interface capability and you can create entire data driven websites and applications that run across most modern browsers, including mobile.

In addition to the integrated development environment (IDE), Google Script comes complete with a manager for organizing scripts, built-in debugging, auto code completion, timed event triggers, and automated revisioning to name a few features. What really caught this author's attention was that everything is web-based. There is no need to download and configure a code editor or transport development files from computer to computer, wasting time resynchronizing files and reconnecting libraries. Simply sign into your Google account and start creating. Google Scripts are written in the JavaScript language version 1.8/ECMA 262 (3rd Edition), so there is no need to compile the code, making application development very fast.

With its own set of libraries, Google Script can interact with most of the services provided by Google, making it the Swiss army knife behind the mainline products. Other application building methods for accessing Google products like App Engine and the gData APIs, offered in many different languages, all require a place for you to develop and deploy your code. With Google Script, you are building the code into the existing Google platform, and that equates a robust experience where your products are inherent in Google's legendary 99.9 percent availability. Because there is no need to have anything more than a basic Internet connected browser, development on this platform is something anyone can get started with, and there is no upfront expense. Google Script is not locked inside Google where it can only talk to Google servers, rather it can communicate through JDBC, JSON, SOAP, and has a `urlFetch` method making it very versatile when communicating across the Web.

At Google I/O 2010, a new feature called UiApp was unveiled, giving Google Script programmers the ability to build custom user interfaces that can run inside a spreadsheet window as a Google Gadget or completely independent in a browser. Talk about earth shattering, a cloud programing platform that can access just about any web-based service and has the ability to create AJAX style web pages? That is noteworthy. One year later, in 2011, additional improvements were added, giving Google Script a drag-and-drop visual editor. This feature reduces the amount of code writing and makes creating an application more approachable for power users with limited coding experience. To date, Google Script is the only way to gain full access to Gmail at the message level.

This book will focus on teaching you how to build powerful web applications using Google Script. It is laid out in sections that explain how the different parts of Google Script work and puts all these together in a series of fully functional applications that you can put to work right away.

Who Should Read This Book

This book is perfect for anyone who wants to extend what can be done with Google Apps but is not ready to dive into the complicated world of the Google Web Tool Kit and Java APIs. You don't have to be a webmaster or programmer to grasp the concepts in this book. Google Script takes care of server configuration, gives you a place to save your projects and allows you to start developing immediately. This book is approachable by anyone with basic coding skills and a fundamental understanding of JavaScript. If you have never used JavaScript, I recommend having a copy of *Head First Java-Script* (O'Reilly) close at hand to help you through concepts like variables, arrays, and objects. All the application examples have highly detailed explanations, so if you are a Google Apps power user, you should not have difficulty grasping the content in this book and writing incredible applications using Google Script.

What You Will Need

You will need a web browser (I recommend Chrome) and any type of Google account. That's it! Google Script is a completely web-based solution that is free and ready for you to start programming today.

Conventions Used in This Book

The following typographical conventions are used in this book:

Italic
> Indicates new terms, URLs, email addresses, filenames, and file extensions.

`Constant width`
> Used for program listings, as well as within paragraphs to refer to program elements such as variable or function names, databases, data types, environment variables, statements, and keywords.

`Constant width bold`
> Shows commands or other text that should be typed literally by the user.

`Constant width italic`
> Shows text that should be replaced with user-supplied values or by values determined by context.

 This icon signifies a tip, suggestion, or general note.

 This icon indicates a warning or caution.

Using Code Examples

This book is here to help you get your job done. In general, you may use the code in this book in your programs and documentation. You do not need to contact us for permission unless you're reproducing a significant portion of the code. For example, writing a program that uses several chunks of code from this book does not require permission. Selling or distributing a CD-ROM of examples from O'Reilly books does require permission. Answering a question by citing this book and quoting example code does not require permission. Incorporating a significant amount of example code from this book into your product's documentation does require permission.

We appreciate, but do not require, attribution. An attribution usually includes the title, author, publisher, and ISBN. For example: "*Google Script: Enterprise Application Essentials* by James Ferreira (O'Reilly). Copyright 2012 James Ferreira, 978-1-449-31852-9."

If you feel your use of code examples falls outside fair use or the permission given above, feel free to contact us at *permissions@oreilly.com*.

Safari® Books Online

Safari Books Online is an on-demand digital library that lets you easily search over 7,500 technology and creative reference books and videos to find the answers you need quickly.

With a subscription, you can read any page and watch any video from our library online. Read books on your cell phone and mobile devices. Access new titles before they are available for print, and get exclusive access to manuscripts in development and post feedback for the authors. Copy and paste code samples, organize your favorites, download chapters, bookmark key sections, create notes, print out pages, and benefit from tons of other time-saving features.

O'Reilly Media has uploaded this book to the Safari Books Online service. To have full digital access to this book and others on similar topics from O'Reilly and other publishers, sign up for free at *http://my.safaribooksonline.com*.

How to Contact Us

Please address comments and questions concerning this book to the publisher:

O'Reilly Media, Inc.
1005 Gravenstein Highway North
Sebastopol, CA 95472
800-998-9938 (in the United States or Canada)
707-829-0515 (international or local)
707-829-0104 (fax)

We have a web page for this book, where we list errata, examples, and any additional information. You can access this page at:

http://www.oreilly.com/catalog/9781449318529

To comment or ask technical questions about this book, send email to:

bookquestions@oreilly.com

For more information about our books, courses, conferences, and news, see our website at *http://www.oreilly.com*.

Find us on Facebook: *http://facebook.com/oreilly*

Follow us on Twitter: *http://twitter.com/oreillymedia*

Watch us on YouTube: *http://www.youtube.com/oreillymedia*

PART I

Understanding Google Script

First Steps in Google Script

What is Google Script and why should you use it to build a web application? Simply put, Google Script is an easy way to figuratively glue Google and other web services together to form one powerful interactive web application. Just ahead, a more in-depth explanation of Google Script and how to use it to enhance existing Google Apps. You will also learn the basics of building an application. This first chapter should get your feet firmly planted on the ground floor of the Google Script development platform and demystify its usage.

Google Script Is...

Google Script is a coding and application development platform built into Google Apps, enabling you to add functionality to spreadsheets, Gmail, Sites, and other services from Google. For example, if your spreadsheet needs a menu item in the tool bar for creating a pivot table, you would write a Google Script that adds it to the menu and performs the task. Because Google Script serves as a backend to other Google services, you will need a spreadsheet or Site to hold the scripts you create. This does not mean that your script will be limited to the spreadsheet or site containing the script. On the contrary, a Google Script can run as a web service without the user ever knowing there is a spreadsheet involved in the interaction. This book will focus extensively on the concept of using Google Script to build applications that present themselves as web services running independently of other interfaces. You will learn how to use Google Script to build apps that run from a spreadsheet, in a browser window or within a Google Site, and from the user's perspective, they will appear to be complete applications such as you might expect when using a web service like Picasa or Amazon.

There are some real advantages to having your scripts (i.e. applications) stored in one of the Google Apps services. Primarily, security is already built-in, meaning you do not need to worry about implementing that component into your application as you would if it were running on a legacy web server needing patches and constant monitoring for malicious attacks. As part of Google Apps, Google Script also allows you the same collaborative development abilities that are part of the Apps suite. What is truly exciting about Google Script is that it is a 100 percent web development environment that requires no transferring of files from computer to computer, backups, revision control, uploads to a production server, updating the development software, or many of the other tedious aspects of development that get in the way of actually writing applications. These parts are all built-in, allowing you to focus on creating products for your business, school, club, or anything that needs to run on the Web.

The UiApp service, which stands for User Interface App, was released in early 2010 as a way to allow developers to collect user input that could be sent back to a script for processing. UiApp uses the Google Web Toolkit (GWT) Widget set as the framework for building an interface. Widgets allow you to create such things as a text box and a Submit button but also more complex items like flex tables and list boxes. Everything you see in a Google Script UI are widgets cleverly arranged within a frame in the page. The only other elements—panels—are the containers that hold all your widgets, and that is truly all there is to the visual part of a Google Script UI. Part III lists every Google Script Widget, including example code. If you are familiar with GWT, you will be right at home creating UIs in Google Script. Never heard of GWT? Don't worry, this book will have you crafting widgets and transversing AJAX with little pain and only a mildly slopping learning curve.

What You Will Get From This Book

By the time you get to the back cover you will have learned all the necessary elements that go into building enterprise applications using Google Script. With this knowledge under your belt, you will be able to create your own applications and take full advantage of your Google hosted services. Your apps will have the ability to recognize and authenticate users and carry out tasks such as displaying custom data from a spreadsheet, data entry, sending emails, and so much more. Have a look at Part II to see the kinds of applications we will be building and let your imagination flow.

Getting Started

Enough preamble, let's dig in!

For the most part, we will be building our scripts in the Google Documents service. To get started with the examples in this chapter, load up Google Docs, *http:docs.google .com* or *http:docs.google.com/a/<your domain>* if you are using a Google Apps account. Create a new Spreadsheet.

In your Spreadsheet, click the Tools menu, then select Script editor, see Figure 1-1.

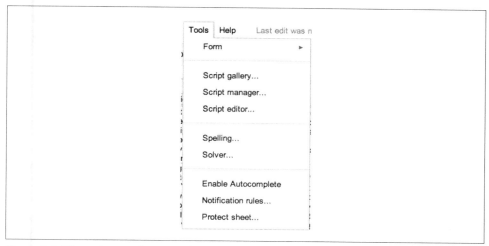

Figure 1-1. The tools menu has several options for managing scripts.

The Google Script editor will open as a new window, see Figure 1-2.

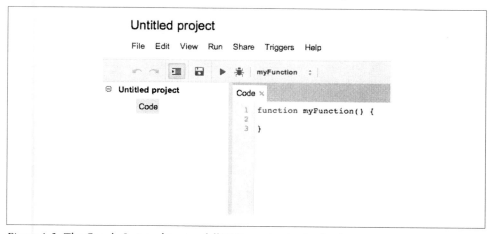

Figure 1-2. The Google Script editor is a full IDE running in the cloud.

Looking Around the Editor

Before writing your first script, let's take a look at some of the features in the Google Script editor. First off you will notice that it looks much like what you already know from Google Documents. Under the File menu are the typical Save, Delete, Rename, Open, Create New File or Project, etc. Also like many of the other Google Apps services, there is a Revisions feature that will allow you to turn back the clock to a point when your code *was* working. (Not that we ever need such features...) Seriously, we often go down the wrong road during development, and revisions can save you hours of trying to get back to a known good point. When launched, a pop-up Revisions box will show what the code looked like in the version you selected.

In the File menu, there are two very important options: "Properties" and "Build a User Interface." Properties makes it possible to store a limited amount of information in Key:Value pairs for use by your script at runtime. Properties can be edited in the box that pops up after clicking the "Properties" option in the File menu, or by using the Properties Service right in your code. Many of the apps in this book will need to sign into non-Google services, and Script Properties is a great place to store something like a password. The Build a User Interface, or the GUI Builder, is one of the tools we will use to create a user interface. This will be covered throughout the book, so just note that this is where you launch it.

Nothing very exciting in the Edit menu, other than "Find Selection," which also incorporates Replace, a good way to globally change the name of a variable. Moving onto the View menu, there are some important points: Execution Transcript and Logs. When a script is run from the editor, the Execution Transcript will list each command as it is run. Using the Execution Transcript, you can see the order that the code is executed, which is helpful in debugging. "Logs" is used along with the Logger Service and allows the writing of information and other notes as a way to track information. This was very useful before the debugger was added and can still be a big help when testing code. I want to reiterate that these features only work from the Editor and will not be of much use debugging in the UiApp when it is run from the browser. Don't worry, there is a whole section to help you debug like a pro.

A quick example of using the Logger:

```
function myFunction(){
  Logger.log('A test of the Log');
}
```

Click Run, and then check in the Log under the View menu.

The Share menu is where access to the script is set and where you will find the Publish option that makes displaying a UI possible. The publishing feature is covered later in the chapter.

Triggers are the automation component that have the ability to run a script at specified times or in certain events, like the submission of a form or when the spreadsheet is edited. Triggers are very useful for tasks such as backing up information at 1 A.M. so you get credit for working hard while fast asleep.

That's about it for the menu. Figure 1-3 shows a few buttons that explain themselves and make for easier access to the most common features.

The Debug option next to Run will bring up a window at the bottom of the code window and show the values of your code as it is executed. It has features for setting break points, stepping in and over parts of code, and will make developing non-UI parts of

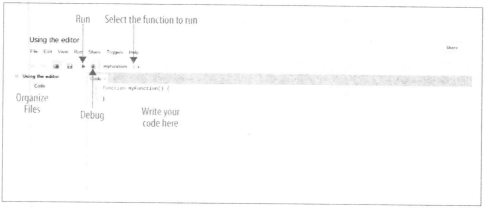

Figure 1-3. Buttons make for easy access to common tasks.

your code much easier. The user documentation on the Google Script website goes into detail on usage of the debugger (*http://code.google.com/googleapps/appsscript/guide _writing_scripts.html*).

Three Ways to Create a UI

There are three ways to create and display a user interface (UI) in Google Script. The first way is in a spreadsheet as a pop-up window; the second, as a web page; and the third as a gadget in a Google sites page.

As you work through this chapter, please note that some of the code in each type of UI is the same and will only be described once as it is first introduced. It would be a good idea to go through all the different UI types to avoid confusion about a certain topic and to gain an understanding of when and why a certain UI type would work better for your application.

Hello UiApp Spreadsheet Integrated

Now that you know your way around the Editor, it is time to write your first script. Keep in mind that all Google Scripts are written entirely in JavaScript and there is no HTML needed to generate the UI. The first type of UI is called "Integrated" because it is going to display as a pop-up window in our spreadsheet. The term "integrated" comes from requiring a spreadsheet to display the UI, but this does not mean that any certain type of UI is more or less integrated than another. It is simply to give you a reference of what we are discussing because the code to display each type differs slightly.

Open the Editor, click File, and select New. In the new script, delete all of the example code, and add the following code:

```
function helloWorld() {
  var mydoc = SpreadsheetApp.getActiveSpreadsheet();
```

```
    var application = UiApp.createApplication().setTitle('Your Title');
    //TODO add your code here
    mydoc.show(application);
}
```

Click Save, and name your script "Hello World Integrated". Now click Run. Switch your browser window to the Spreadsheet view, and you will see an empty UI window with the title "Hello World" at the top.

 The core of all Integrated UiApps and the components to make the UI display:

```
UiApp.createApplication();
show(application);
```

Diving into the code

All Google Scripts start with a function; when using the integrated UI, you can name your function almost anything you like:

```
function <name>()
```

 The function names doGet, doPost, onEdit, onInstall, and onOpen are special reserved functions and should not be used as names for custom functions you create that are not performing these specific operations.

Here we use the Google Script Spreadsheets Service (*http://code.google.com/googleapps/appsscript/service_spreadsheet.html*) to create an object called "mydoc" that represents the current spreadsheet:

```
var mydoc = SpreadsheetApp.getActiveSpreadsheet();
```

The following line creates the UiApp object, which contains all the methods for creating UIs:

```
var app = UiApp.createApplication();
```

When using a spreadsheet, you need to insert the script into it by using the show method:

```
mydoc.show(application);
```

Time to get something for you to look at. Find the line starting with //TODO and replace it with the following code block:

```
var helloWorldLabel = app.createLabel('My first Google Script UI');
app.add(helloWorldLabel);
```

To display information on the UI, you will need a widget. In this case, a simple label will be created, which is a widget that only takes text in its argument and shows inline. Labels can be styled with CSS to give you all sorts of creative options. To make the Label widget appear in the UI, it needs to be added to the UiApp object by calling the add method and using the variable name in the methods argument.

Run the script and switch your browser to the window containing the spreadsheet. Figure 1-4 shows the UI displayed in a spreadsheet. There are endless possibilities for why you might want to pop up an interface for the user: data entry, choosing information from another service like Contacts, or running a script requesting additional information are just a few examples.

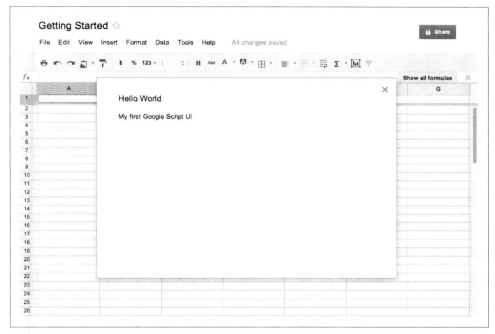

Figure 1-4. UI running inside a spreadsheet

Integrated Versus Standalone

One of the most exciting features of the UI Service is that it can run all by itself without the need to open a spreadsheet. This is accomplished by publishing the script, which creates an access point through a special Google URL. There are several options when publishing, such as restricting access to anyone but you or opening up the UI so that anyone visiting the URL can run it. Publishing does not, however, allow visitor access to your code; that is controlled by the sharing in the spreadsheet or site. This means you can create your application and the code will stay safely secured.

One important thing to remember is that a script running as a published web service will always run under the creator's account and will have access to the services to which he has granted access. Therefore, if your script lists all the emails in your Inbox and you make it public, anyone visiting the URL will see your Inbox not rather than his own.

Running the script as your account can be a benefit because you can set the spreadsheet sharing to limit access and then control what a UI viewer sees about the data while still allowing input into the spreadsheet. There will be more on this concept later when we start putting together real-world apps in Part II.

One limitation to having the script run as you, the creator, is that you will not be able to directly access a user's account from the built-in classes. For example, if your application needs to access the user's Contacts service, it will not work that way. You don't have that user to user access in Google Apps, so it does not work in Google Script either. Later in the book we will cover how to handle this problem using two-legged OAuth.

 In the Integrated UI spreadsheet version of a Google Script, your users have the same access as the spreadsheet, so unlike the standalone UI, where a script runs under your account, the Integrated UI will run as the user's account.

While I present these differences of the two UiApp styles as hurdles, there are some very good reasons to have access restricted in this way. Fortunately, these security features don't limit us in building apps, but they add certain complexities that need to be considered.

Creating a Standalone UI

The second type of UI application is referred to as standalone because the UI is accessed from a special URL hosted on Google's cloud. There is no need for a spreadsheet to use the standalone UI but you can build this type of UI in a spreadsheet or in any of the Google services where the script editor is available. The URL can be made public allowing DNS mapping to your domain. For example, *http://Your_Great_App.domain.com*.

Open the script editor, select File→New. Replace the myFunction code with:

```
function doGet(e) {
  var application = UiApp.createApplication();
  //Your Code
  return application;
}
```

 The standalone UiApp will be the most commonly used style in this book because it has the ability to run as a gadget in a Sites page or as its own independent page.

The first difference from the Integrated UI version is that we must have a doGet function for the UiApp window manager to grab when the standalone URL is loaded in a browser. This is analogous to the entry point you might use in GWT. `doGet` is the starting point for loading visible elements in the standalone UI.

The visual part of the UI is created using the UiApp class that will create an object for display. You don't need to have a widget to present visual information to the user if your script's purpose is to simply perform a task when the URL is loaded. This is accomplished by passing values in the URL parameters and will be covered in Chapter 8. Even if you are only collecting information and don't have content to display, it is good practice to put a message of some kind on the page for the user:

```
var application = UiApp.createApplication()
```

To get the UI to display a widget on the page you must return the UiApp instance:

```
return application;
```

Think of it this way, when you load the UiApp's URL, a Google server hosting your code looks for and runs the `doGet` function. If there is no return value for `doGet`, you will not see anything on the page. If you have not yet guessed, all Google Scripts run on the server side and the interaction you see is accomplished through remote procedure calls (RPC).

To display some text on the page, create a label and add it to the `application` object in the same way you did for the Integrated UI type:

```
var label = app.createLabel('Nothing but Web');
app.add(label);
```

That is all there is to making a basic UI page. Click Save, and name your script **Stand-alone Web Service**.

Publishing a script

To make the UI available, it will need to be published to the Web. This is Google's way of saying that a special URL has been created and the UI will be served from there. It is not public unless you make it so.

Click the Share menu and select "Publish as service..." as shown in Figure 1-5.

Figure 1-6 shows the "Publish as service..." option where you can choose the level of access you would like visitors to have. The options differ depending on whether you are using a Google or Google Apps account. The last setting—"Allow anyone to invoke the service"—will give access to any visitor that has a Google account. When you check this option, an additional choice will appear allowing you to select "Anonymous access," meaning the script is fully open to the Web and no sign-in is required.

The "yada yada" Google refers to is a serious warning. When you build a standalone application, it will run as you and it will have access to anything you have given it permission to see. For example, be careful not to publish the contents of your email Inbox to everyone on the Web.

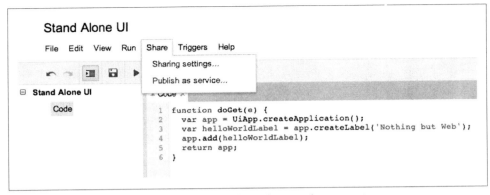

Figure 1-5. The Share menu has an option to allow others to edit your script.

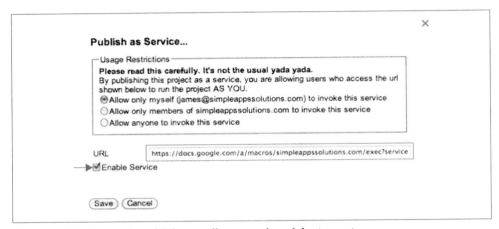

Figure 1-6. Settings on the publish page allow a number of sharing options.

Once you have chosen the level of access, check the Enable Service box and copy the URL in the box. This is the special URL for the page where this UI is being hosted. If you forget it, simply open this dialog and copy again. Click Save and open a new tab in your browser. Paste the URL in the address bar and load the page. You should now see your UI displaying the text from the label created earlier.

Congratulations! You have just created your first Google Script UI Web Service. Not much of a "service" yet, but as you can see, it takes very little effort to get an application pushed out to a web interface. What you might have missed is everything that is going on here, which can be a good thing. For one, you did not need to create an HTML page, or figure out how to FTP to a web server somewhere to upload files. To that extent, you also didn't need to purchase and install a web server or buy a domain. Google Script gives you the ability to write your application entirely in JavaScript and then takes care of the rest of the details. I don't want to say it gets easier from here, but this is the foundation; after this, the functionality of providing a service has more to do with adding widgets and filling them with data. There is no more that needs to be done to create the UI service or web page. Maintenance, access, and version tracking is integrated, which means you can focus on the code.

Making Google Sites Interactive

To this point, Google Documents has been used to work with the Script Editor and create UIs. However, the Editor is also available in the Google Sites service, allowing UI scripts to be inserted as gadgets appearing on the pages in your sites. This is tremendously exciting for Google Sites users because it means having the ability to create complex interactions that would normally require code hosted on a server somewhere else. For example, a business could feature products with color options that the user can change to see a different look, an HR department application might allow training sign up pages that bring back live calendar results or a school could host an educational game for students. These are just a few examples, but the options are virtually limitless.

Using the GUI Builder

In this section, you will learn how to open the Script Editor from a Google Site, create a UI using the GUI Builder, and place the script as a gadget in a Sites page. Time to load up a Google Site and do some more scripting.

From a Sites page, click the "More actions" menu on the upper-right. Select "Manage site," then, on the left, select "Apps Scripts." Figure 1-7 shows the Script Manager that will list all of your scripts. Well, there are no scripts yet so let's do something about that. Click "Add new script" to launch the Script Editor. Look familiar? This is the same Script Editor we used in the spreadsheet, only the script storage location has changed to Google Sites. Click Save and name your script **GUI Builder**.

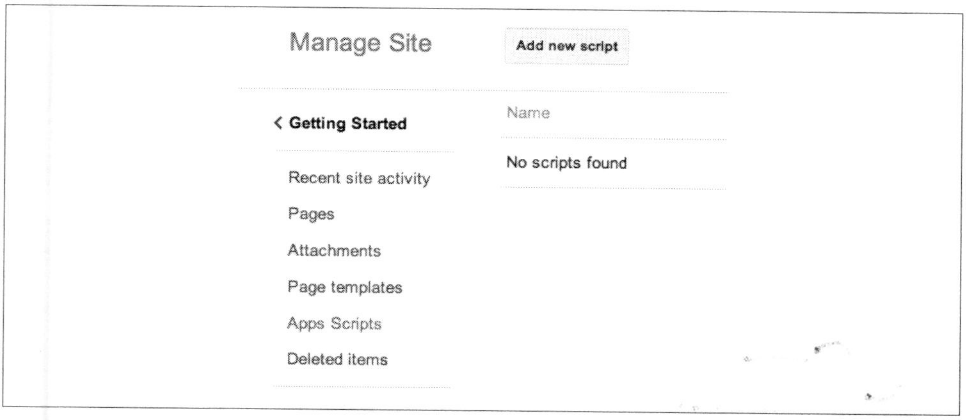

Manage Site   Add new script

‹ **Getting Started**   Name

Recent site activity   No scripts found

Pages

Attachments

Page templates

Apps Scripts

Deleted items

Figure 1-7. Sites has a Script Manager to help keep you organized.

There is not a concept of an integrated application for a site like in a spreadsheet, so use the "Creating a Standalone UI" on page 10 style of UI any time you write scripts for a site. In the last two examples, you have handwritten the code that created a label widget to display on the page. It is important you have this skill as your apps grow in complexity, but in some cases you just need to quickly arrange text boxes and buttons on the page. Let me now introduce you to the GUI Builder, Figure 1-8, which gives you a way to build a UI without writing any code. You invoke it by clicking "File" and selecting "Build a User Interface."

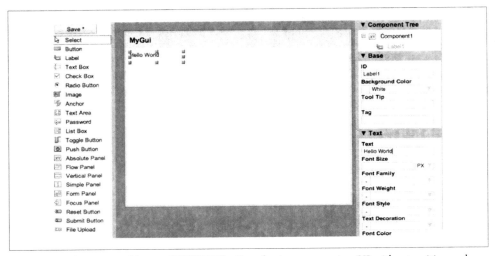

Figure 1-8. The GUI Builder is a WYSIWYG editor, letting you create a UI without writing code.

The GUI Builder is a WYSIWYG (What You See Is What You Get) editing tool that will let you create your interface by simply dragging elements into the MyGUI window.

Continuing on our theme, drag a label widget from the left into the compose window and position it near the top-left. Once you drop the label, you will see its attributes appear on the right. In the box below the word Text, change Label1 to Hello World. You will see that the label in the compose window has updated its text as you type.

Click Save, name your GUI MyGui, and return to the Script Editor.

To load the GUI you just created, use app.loadComponent("MyGui") and add it to the UiApp instance. The code looks like this:

```
function doGet(e) {
  var application = UiApp.createApplication();
  app.add(app.loadComponent("MyGui")); // name of the saved Gui
  return application;
}
```

→ & Publish as Webapp

Save your script and head back to the page on your site where you would like to display your new UI. In Page Edit mode, click Insert, as shown in Figure 1-9, and select Apps Script Gadget.

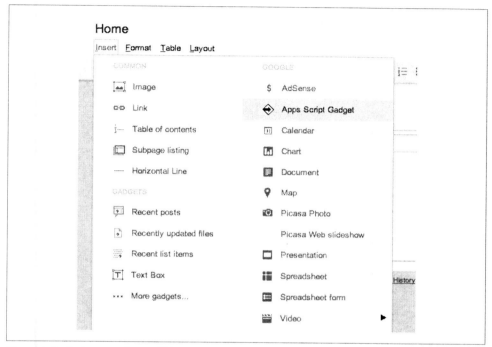

Figure 1-9. Gadgets can be used like any other item that inserts in a Google Site.

Choose your script and click Select. Now you are presented with a panel with options that control the sharing and the look of the gadget. We will cover these options in detail later; for now, click Save. Click Save again to close the Page Editor, and you will see your gadget live on the page.

Up and Walking

Here we are at the end of Chapter 1, and a lot of ground has been covered. Starting with a description of where to find the Google Script Editor and what one might use it for, then progressing on to creating a new script. After that, you learned how to make your UI appear integrated in a Google Spreadsheet and then as an independent web page. Lastly, you accessed the Script Editor from a Google Site and learned about the easy-to-use WYSIWYG GUI Builder that allowed you to make a gadget without writing much code, then used the UI as a gadget on a Google Sites page. You should now have your feet under you and be able to find your way around the Google Script service.

In Chapter 2, you will continue mastering Google Script by learning about helpful ways to arrange your development environment and how to debug UI code.

Setting Up Your Development Environment

When developing a UI in Google Script, you will often load the UI in a browser to see how code is rendered on the page. The GUI builder will certainly help you see a draft of your UI, but it does not load the live data. Among the several ways of displaying the UI during development, it is best to use the standalone web page. The reason for this is that each time a change is made in the script, proofing that change only requires reloading the UI published page.

The Script Editor has a built-in debugger that can help when you are working up the processing elements. For example, you would like to retrieve some data from a SOAP service and parse the XML. The debugger will allow you to set break points so you can step through the code and review values throughout the process.

Once you start using interactive elements in the UI like a click handler, you will not be able to use the debugger. This is because the frontend of the UI is loaded into the browser and therefore independent of the Script Editor. Later in this chapter, we will introduce an error catching method that will help you find problems in your code.

Most developers like to have an arrangement of code, live view, and console output like what you have in the Eclipse IDE. Figure 2-1 shows a layout of three browser windows that effectively create an IDE look for Google Script.

To create this setup, open a new window for the Script Editor, a spreadsheet used for error checking, and the web service page. Now move and size them. You can get some more space by hiding toolbars that you don't need.

How to Debug and Test

Each time you save a script, Google will run through the code and make sure there are no syntax errors. That does not mean the Editor will tell you if a variable is not defined or a web service could not be reached. It will tell you that you forgot a closing bracket

Figure 2-1. Arranging windows on your desktop can save time during development.

or added an extra quote. This error checking is displayed at the top of the page in red with the error and line number where the issue occurs. When you run the script from the Editor, the same notification will show runtime errors such as undefined variables.

UiApps must run in a page, spreadsheet, or gadget, which means that runtime errors can't be shown in the Script Editor. Next we will look at three ways of displaying errors for development and production.

Handling Errors and Breaks

Like most object-oriented programing languages, Google Script uses the try/catch statement to work with errors at runtime. It is important to know that the browser will return errors as well, however, one can get more detail using try/catch.

Let's see this in practice: open the Script Editor and create a new script. Save the script, name it **Errors**, and then publish the UI as explained in Chapter 1.

Copy and paste the buggy code below into your Errors script:

```
function doGet() {
  var app = UiApp.createApplication();
  var x=t;  return app;
}
```

Now reload the UI page and note the error: "ReferenceError: "t" is not defined." Not much of a problem in our five lines of code to see where the problem is, but what if our code was 5,000 lines long?

Let's try that again using a try/catch statement and a UI element to display it:

```
function doGet() {
  var app = UiApp.createApplication();
  var message = app.createLabel('').setId('message')
      .setVisible(false).setStyleAttribute('color', 'red');
  app.add(message);
  try{
    var x=t;
  }catch(e){
      message.setText(e.name + ' on line: ' + e.lineNumber + ' -> ' +
          e.message).setVisible(true);
  }
  return app;
}
```

Reload the UI again, and we have a new message: "ReferenceError on line: 9 → "t" is not defined."

What we have created is a known stable wrapper for any code we insert between the try and catch that will give detailed information about errors that occur at runtime. Next we will extend this container and set breakpoints to help understand what is happening during a run.

Break and Report

Sometimes you need to test out what a service or other operation is returning in order to build the UI. Other times an error may be because of the values being fed to the failing code. When we talk about "breaking the code," what we mean is that you will stop the run at a certain point so you have an opportunity to see what values exist at that given point.

Following the example above, let's test the value of x before setting it to the undefined "t" value. Replace the code between the try/catch with the following:

```
...
var x=5;
message.setText("Value of x is: " + x).setVisible(true);
return app;
x=t;
...
```

Remember that JavaScript is a top-down language. Therefore, each line runs one after the other. Certainly you can run a function that may be at the very end of the code and then come back to the top, but the order of execution will always be line-by-line, there is no go-to line 9 in JavaScript.

In the new code, the value of x is set to 5. Next we will write to the message label what x is now. The error of t not being defined still exists but will not be executed because the app is returned (breaks) before that line runs. Therefore, we will only see the message: Value of x is: 5.

Production Error Logging

Debugging is essential during your development, but keep in mind it will only catch what *you* expect, and your users will always find ways to use your product in ways you would not have thought possible. This section will discuss how to keep track of problems in your apps that are out in the wild, untamed user realm.

The concept is simple: use a try/catch statement like what was done in "Handling Errors and Breaks" on page 18, but with the twist of logging each error on a spreadsheet. I would like to note that if you are the twitchy type, you can also have errors emailed directly to you as they occur. I don't recommend this because it is hard to sift through emails looking to see the order of things when a spreadsheet organizes the failures in the order they occurred. If you want an email to let you know things have gone awry, you can always set the spreadsheet notification feature to send an email.

Here's the setup:

1. Create a new spreadsheet and rename a sheet **errors**.

   This will be the place for logging errors. You must make sure that the account running the script has editor permissions.

2. Get the Spreadsheet ID from the URL.

   Example:

   https://spreadsheets0.google.com/a/example.com/spreadsheet/ccc?key=0Aq1-MXh5TOc3NVE&hl=en_US#gid=0

   The 0Aq1-MXh5TOc3NVE part is your spreadsheet's ID.

3. Modify the code from "Handling Errors and Breaks" on page 18 by inserting the following code:

```
}catch(error){
  var errorSheet = SpreadsheetApp.openById('your sheet
ID').getSheetByName('errors');
  var cell = errorSheet.getRange('A1').offset(errorSheet.getLastRow(),0);
  cell.setValue("function doGet: " + error);
}
```

Now when you run the script, errors will be written to the spreadsheet row by row. Adding time stamps can also help identify why something may be failing.

Wrapping Up

In this chapter, you learned several ways to debug your code and keep track of problems in your script after deployment. Remember that users like to have useful information to give you when things have gone wrong. A generic error at the top of the page or worse—seemingly nothing at all—will only frustrate the user and lessen the usefulness of your app.

You should always keep an eye out for places in your code where several things need to be processed and a failure would kill the whole run. Employ the try/catch in these cases so that one failure is reported while the remaining tasks complete.

Building an Interface

What's in a UI?

A User Interface, or UI, is what you see when you turn on a computer. It may be an action-packed blockbuster movie or a single flashing green ">", but one thing is for sure, this is your way to interact with the machine. When we talk about building a UI, we are typically speaking of the part that your user will need to interact with your application. Text to read, pictures to look at, boxes to type in, and buttons to push are what we call widgets. To keep these elements from dropping to the bottom of the screen in a big pile, we will place them in panels. A panel is a container that allows the widgets to be generally arranged on the screen. You can have panels within panels and widgets inside widgets, or even panels inside widgets. The combinations are virtually unlimited (pun intended). Part III contains examples of widgets and panels available in the UiApp.

When we build a UI in Google Apps Script, there are three ways to present the UI to the user: in a spreadsheet, in a Google Site as a gadget, or as a web page, which we call standalone. Please see Chapter 1 for a detailed description of each UI display type. For this chapter, the focus will be on the standalone UI.

When you publish your stand alone UI it gets a Google hosted web page with a little bit of HTML and some JavaScript wrapped around your code. Google Script uses GWT technology to send your script to the browser as highly optimized JavaScript. This process increases security and facilitates compatibility across major browsers thus lessening the possibility your UI won't display properly. To put it simply, you write the code and it just works.

It Starts with doGet()

In order to display a UI in the standalone or Sites gadget, you must have a function called doGet with a UiApp instance inside. When using a spreadsheet integrated UI, you can call your function anything you like because of the way Google has done the wrapper.

In Figure 3-1, we can see the arrangement of several widgets and panels. The UiApp itself acts much like a vertical panel. When adding widgets—in this case, Submit buttons—directly to the UiApp, they stack vertically on the screen. Here is how that looks as code:

```
var app = UiApp.createApplication(); // the UI instance
app.add(app.createButton('Submit')); // adding a button directly
app.add(app.createButton('Submit'));
// a different method, same result
var button = app.createButton('Submit'); //creates a button object
app.add(button); //adding the button object
return app;
```

Remember that the UiApp is the class object from which you will create everything seen in the UI. In this book, the UI instance of UiApp will almost always be referred to as *app*. You must always return *app* or nothing will show in the UI. If you don't see your widgets, it is likely you forgot to add them to *app* at some point.

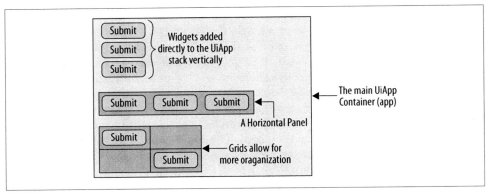

Figure 3-1. Each panel has different ways to arrange the widgets.

After adding the three buttons, a horizontal panel is added to *app* and three more buttons are then added to the horizontal panel. This panel is going to act more like typing words in a text editor. Each time you add a letter, it goes to the right of the letter preceding until you get to the end of a line, then the letters skip down and continue along. This is how a horizontal panel works as well.

```
var horizontalPanel = UiApp.createHorizontalPanel();
app.add(horizontalPanel);

horizontalPanel.add(app.createButton('Submit'));
horizontalPanel.add(app.createButton('Submit'));
var button = app.createButton('Submit');
horizontalPanel.add(button);
```

As you can see, adding widgets to the horizontal panel is exactly like adding them to *app*. Because the horizontal panel now contains many widgets, you might think of it as a component. The relationship is that of parents and children: the UiApp is the parent and the horizontal panel is a child. The buttons at the top are also children of the UiApp, and the buttons in the horizontal panel are grandchildren. Some of the buttons are aunts and there may be at least one second cousin. Is this way too confusing? That is the problem with nesting panels and widgets many levels deep.

Sometimes it is simpler to use a grid for your layout. The advantage here is that you can add widgets or panels to a given cell location. Figure 3-1 shows a grid with one button in the upper-left and another in the lower-right. To get the same effect using panels would take one horizontal, two vertical, each containing two more vertical panels. That's a grand total of seven panels compared to one grid. Adding to a grid is a little different because you will need to specify the cell you would like to add your widget.

```
var grid = app.createGrid(2,2); // 2 cells tall and 2 wide
app.add(grid);

var button1 = app.createButton('Submit');
var button2 = app.createButton('Submit');

grid.setWidget(0,0, button1);
grid.setWidget(1,1, button2);
```

Take careful note that grids are zero based when adding elements.

There you have it, the basics of presenting some objects to the user. Next up, we will build a real interface that you have likely used on many web pages.

Contact Me

Sales just called; they want you to add a "Contact Me" form on the website so the company can email news updates when something big happens. You could simply fire up the built-in form tool from Google Documents and insert one question with a text box, but there are a few things you don't like. First, the Google form has extra information about it being a Google form, thus taking extra space on the page. Second, you don't want the full page "submitted" notification that takes the customer away from the site to pop up. If you don't know already, verification is not built into the stock Google forms, and you would really like to lessen the effort on the backend to weed out jokers that didn't enter something that looks like an email. No problem, doing what you want in Google Apps is what Google Script is all about.

Thinking about your UI, you decide there will need to be a label to tell the user what to do, a text box for them to enter an email address, and a button to submit the change. You would like to verify that they entered an email and provide some kind feedback if they did not. Finally it would be nice to display that something happened when they pushed the button by saying, "Thank you."

In this chapter, we will create the UI using two different methods. In Chapter 4, we will add the actions that perform the work once Submit is clicked. You will need a Google

Site to complete this example. Both are provided in Google Apps so you are already setup.

Using the GUI Builder

The GUI Builder is an incredibly fast way to get going in building UIs in Google Script. Why, you ask? One word: WYSIWYG. Well, technically that would be an acronym of seven powerful words: What You See Is What You Get. Not that you aren't used to this, after all any word processor today is a WYSIWYG (pronounced *wiz-ee-wig*). Let's open the Script Editor from your Site Management page and create a new script.

Click File and select "Build a user interface". The GUI Builder opens in a new window. See Figure 1-8.

In the center, you will find the application window, the one that says MyGui. This is the space where you will construct your UI. One real advantage to using the UI Builder is that it displays your widgets just as they will look in the browser you are using to develop. This will save you a lot of time not having to make changes in the code and reloading the app in the browser.

Building a UI in the GUI Builder is simply a matter of dragging widgets from the left side into the center pane, and arranging them in the application window. You will also note that widgets can be drawn by first selecting a widget and then clicking and dragging in the application window. After it's placed, each widget has blue handles (See Figure 3-2) to change its size; you can move these handles whenever you like. On the right, there's a panel that gives detailed control over the widget that is currently selected. Here, the GUI Builder really shines as it will only allow you to set valid parameters for the widget you are working with.

Let's start creating our Contact Me app by dragging over a flow panel and dropping it in the upper-left corner. Next grab a label and drag it over to the flow panel. You will see a blue box indicating where it is going in the panel once you drop it. On the right, in the Properties panel, find Text and change label1 to **Enter your email to sign up**. You will see that the text in the label widget has updated with the new text.

Now drag a text box and place it below the label; now grab a button and place it right next to the text box. You can clear the text from the text box by deleting everything from the Text property. Change the text box Id and Name to **textBox**.

Finally, drag over a label and place it below the form. Delete the Text and change the ID to **info**.

Select the Flow panel and drag the right blue handle to just to where the button ends. Now in the Properties panel change the ID of the Flow panel to **mainPanel**. See Figure 3-3.

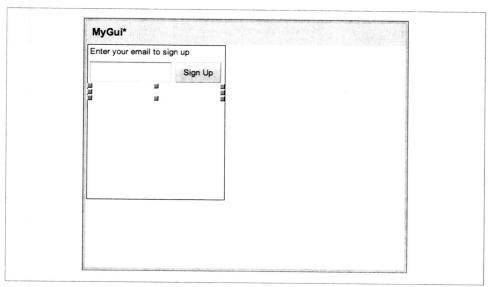

Figure 3-2. Blue markers tell you which item is selected.

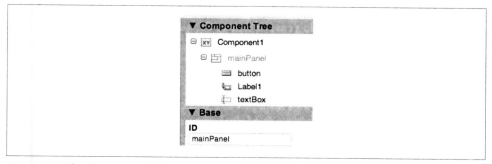

Figure 3-3. The elements and their properties are listed on the right side of the GUI Builder

Click the button widget and change the text property to read: **Sign up**. Now your button face text says something useful. Change the button ID to **button**. You may want to drag the corners of the widgets around a bit to make them look just right.

 When creating UIs in the GUI Builder, keep in mind that it renders its build view just as it would if the code was live on the Web. This means that you can be sure that whatever you create will look good in the browser you are using. If you use a browser that lacks certain features, those things will not be available to you as choices in the GUI Builder.

Time to test it out. Switch windows back to the Script Editor, delete the default function, insert the code below, and save. Figure 3-4 shows the UI loaded on the page.

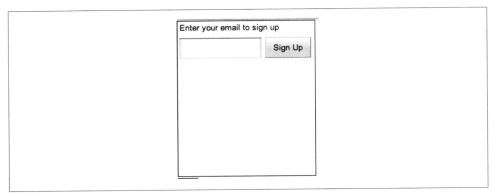

Figure 3-4. The UI looks the same in your browser as it does in the GUI Builder

```
function doGet() {
  var app = UiApp.createApplication();
  app.add(app.loadComponent("MyGui"));
  return app;
}
```

Now publish the script from the Share menu as described in "Publishing a script" on page 11. Paste your published script URL in a new browser window and load.

That was certainly easy and contained only five lines of actual code. Granted, it doesn't do anything, but we will be taking care of that in Chapter 4. Next we are going to look at how to code the UI without the GUI Builder.

Handcoding a GUI

The GUI Builder is the perfect tool for a job like what we have been working with so far, and it certainly makes quick work of designing a UI. However, as your scripts become more complex you will need to have the ability to write the code that creates many layers of user interaction. This may mean starting out with the GUI Builder but then switching out panels and widgets as needed to load different views in your app. Also, learning the ropes of coding the UI will give you a deeper understanding of how the UiApp works.

Create a fresh new script and add the basics, like this:

```
function doGet() {
  var app = UiApp.createApplication();
  //Your code goes here
  return app;
}
```

Go ahead and publish the script and load up a page with the published URL for testing. All of the following code will go where it says *//Your code goes here*.

Create a vertical panel to hold the widgets:

```
var mainPanel = app.createVerticalPanel().setId('mainPanel');
```

The object `mainPanel` is a widget from the UiApp class. There is one more thing, setting the ID of elements (`setId`) is a good habit to get into and will be critical in Chapter 4, when we wire up the interaction.

Next add the new panel to app so it becomes part of the UI:

```
app.add(mainPanel);
```

If you load the UI page now it will appear empty aside from the vertical panel. Now we will need a label to give the user some instructions:

```
mainPanel.add(app.createLabel('Enter your email to sign up'));
```

In this case, we can just add the label right onto the `mainPanel`. Go ahead and reload the UI page to make sure everything is working up to this point. If this was going to be a more complex script, now would be a good time to add some error checking as we discussed in Chapter 2. However, this is a very short script, and I will try to keep you from getting lost.

The next part has two widgets side by side: the text box that collects the email address and the button to save the information. However, if you add these like we did the label, they will be stacked up vertically on the page. Therefore, to get the look we want we will need to add something else. A horizontal panel should do the trick:

```
var form = app.createHorizontalPanel();
mainPanel.add(form);
```

With the horizontal panel added below the instructions label, we can now add widgets; they will line up across the page instead of down.

Next create a text box and set its name and ID so it can be accessed later by handlers:

```
var email = app.createTextBox().setName('textBox').setId('textBox');
form.add(email);
```

Now the button will be created and added to the horizontal panel, which lines it up to the right of the text box:

```
var button = app.createButton('Sign up');
form.add(button);
```

When you create the button, you have a chance to set the text on the face of the button. This could also be done later with setText(String).

The last element is a label to give the user some feedback. This will not be needed until after the user has clicked the button, so it is hidden by setting visibility to `false`:

```
var info = app.createLabel().setVisible(false).setId('info');
mainPanel.add(info);
```

Well, that wasn't too hard was it? Reload the UI page, and you should see that your coding skills have paid off in creating a UI from scratch that looks like what you created in the section on using the GUI Builder:

```
function doGet() {
  var app = UiApp.createApplication();

  var mainPanel = app.createVerticalPanel().setId('mainPanel');
  app.add(mainPanel);

  mainPanel.add(app.createLabel('Enter your email to sign up'));

  var form = app.createHorizontalPanel();
  mainPanel.add(form);

  var email = app.createTextBox().setName('textBox').setId('textBox');
  form.add(email);

  var button = app.createButton('Sign up');
  form.add(button);

  var info = app.createLabel().setVisible(false).setId('info');
  mainPanel.add(info);

  //Save for Validation

  //Save for handler

  return app;
}
```

There you have it, two ways to make a UI. The GUI Builder is certainly faster and much easier to work in for this simple app, but I think it is important for you to see how everything is written out. Knowing this will help you as we start wiring up the button and text box to make it work.

CHAPTER 4

Adding Actions

In Chapter 3, you began creating an application to collect email addresses from visitors who would like you to contact them about whatever it is that you do. The only problem is that clicking your "Sign Up" button doesn't do anything. In this chapter, we will add actions to that button to store the visitor's email address, thank them if they entered an email address, and ask them to try again if they didn't.

Handling a Handler

To make a button work it needs a handler. However, buttons are not the only widgets that can have a handler, and clicking on something is not the only handler type. For example, a text box may have a handler that responds to pressing the Enter key, or a list box sometimes needs to fill a second list for situations like choosing a city after the state has been selected. In that case, we might use an onChange handler. In more advanced UIs, mouse handlers, like "over" and "off," can create rich user interaction by displaying information before a selection is made. It's also important to note that a widget can have more than one handler. When you have a process that may take some time, like receiving data from a web service or uploading files from the hard drive, it's a good idea to show a progress indicator to the user after the click something.

In this chapter, we will keep things simple and only work with the onClick handler to provide action for our simple form.

Some of the handlers in the UiApp:

- BlurHandler
- ChangeHandler
- ClickHandler
- CloseHandler
- Command
- InitializeHandler

- FocusHandler
- KeyHandler
- LoadHandler
- MouseHandler
- SelectionHandler
- ScrollHandler
- SubmitHandler
- ValueChangeHandler

Anatomy of a Handler

You can create a handler like any other element in the UI by calling on the UiApp class to create what you need. While you can attach a handler directly to a widget using the `.add` statement, we will create the handler here by loading it into a variable. This is a common practice because it makes the code more readable, but like most things in programming it's not always the best solution. Later in the book you will learn techniques where attaching the handler directly is preferred.

This is how a handler is created:

```
var handler = app.createServerHandler('contactMe');
```

What we have done is created an object, the handler, using the call `createServerHandler`. In the past, Google Script had many types of button handlers, but now these have been condensed into a single do all server handler. This server handler acts like a click handler used for submit buttons and requires a full button cycle (Down and Up) to execute. That way if the user has pressed down, but then decides she was not ready, she can drag off the button, let go, and the button will not execute.

Handlers have the ability to take a function argument on creation, as we have here in specifying `'contactMe'`, which is the name of the function we will be creating later in the chapter to perform the work. You can also add the function later by using:

```
handler.setCallbackFunction('contactMe');
```

You might be wondering about that method having the word "callback" in it, which leads us to a very important point in the UiApp.

The Concept of the Callback

When your app needs to do something—like update information on the screen, add data to a spreadsheet, or send an email—it performs what is known as a Remote Procedure Call, or RPC for short. An RPC includes sending code to the server for processing and having the server send back the results. I am sure that Java developers are pulling their hair out at this simplistic definition of RPC, but for what you need to know in Google Script, this about covers it.

The function we specified `'contactMe'`—we will create that soon—is what the server is going to do with the information we send. In our case, we are going to need to update the UI with some feedback for the visitor and that means those elements must get passed to the server in the handler. Certainly you could pass just one widget, but in most cases you will need to access many parts of the UI. For example, we will want to get the input from the text box and update the info label. If you look back on the code we created in Chapter 3, there was a panel to hold the widgets that we gave an ID. It turns out that when you pass an object like a panel or other widget in the handler, that also passes all of the widgets and panels that have been added to it. If you need an HTML reference to visualize the process, you can think of those as child elements.

Here is how objects are passed in a handler:

```
handler.addCallbackElement(mainPanel);
```

But wait, there is a difference here if you are using the GUI Builder. Because the GUI Builder stores its information in the builder, you need to use the `getElementById` call. Therefore, instead of using only the variable name `'mainPanel'`, you would call it like this:

```
app.getElementById('mainPanel');
```

There will be more on this later in the chapter, but for now just note that there is a difference.

Now your 'contactMe' function will have access to both the text box and label widgets. To make this more concrete (and sorry for beating you over the head with this but it is really important to get this now), you are essentially passing the whole `mainPanel` to the server, the server is making some changes and then replacing it with those changes made.

That's all there is to creating a handler; now all that is left is to attach the handler to the widget of our choosing. In this example, we will attach it to our Sign Up button:

```
button.addClickHandler(handler);
```

Or if you are using the GUI Builder:

```
app.getElementById('button').addClickHandler(handler);
```

For reference, here is the whole block of code if you handcoded:

```
var handler = app.createServerClickHandler('contactMe');
  handler.addCallbackElement(mainPanel);
  button.addClickHandler(handler);
```

And if you used the GUI Builder:

```
var handler = app.createServerClickHandler('contactMe');
  handler.addCallbackElement(app.getElementById('mainPanel'));
  app.getElementById('button').addClickHandler(handler);
```

Functions Are Where the Action Happens

Applications built for the UiApp have four basic types of functions: doGet, which you are familiar with; doPost, which you will learn about later; functions that return values directly; and functions that are intended to be used via a handler. They aren't really that different, however, *when* you use them can be important. For example, you always need doGet to display the UI in a gadget, and if you are using a form panel, you will likely need a doPost function.

When you operate a function using a handler and your intent is to update the UI, you must call on the active UI and return it at the end of the processing. Here is what that looks like:

```
function contactMe(e){
    var app = UiApp.getActiveApplication();
    //code here
    return app;
}
```

Notice the (e) in the function arguments. That will be the variable that contains the information we passed in the handler. To get at that information, we will use the property parameter where the information is stored and the name we gave the object. For us that is "textBox" so:

```
var email = e.parameter.textBox
```

I have shown the value loaded in a variable email to help you make the connection as to what we are accessing. Later in this chapter we will send that email address to a Google spreadsheet for storage, but for now let's look at returning some information to the user. Because we loaded the active UiApp into the variable app we can call on elements by their ID.

Let me pause for a second here and cover something that really confuses people. You can set values, add widgets, and change the attributes of elements from a function using an ID, but you can't get their values by ID. To get a value, you must pass it through the handler and use e.parameter.<name>. That also means you need to set the name of the element. This goes back to when we discussed RPC and how that works.

To give the user, and you as well, some indication that the button works, we will set the value of the text box to nothing and add a label that says "Thank you."

Replace "//code here" with the following lines:

```
app.getElementById('textBox').setValue('').setStyleAttribute("color", "black");
app.getElementById('info').setText('Thank you!').setStyleAttribute("color", "black");
```

The getElementById part will call on the ID of those elements passed in the callback and allow you to act on them. For the text box, we set the value to an empty string and then we call on the info label to set a new text value. After clicking the button, the contactMe function will run and update the UI.

Save your file, and refresh your UI browser window to load in the new code. Now type anything into the text box and click the button. You should see the text box clear and your "thank you" appear. Congratulations, you are now using AJAX.

A few small problems: the value did not go anywhere and you can type in anything you want. Let's solve the email verification part first.

Here is the contactMe function all together:

```
function contactMe(e){
 var app = UiApp.getActiveApplication();

 app.getElementById('textBox').setValue('').setStyleAttribute("color", "black");
 app.getElementById('info').setText('Thank you!').setStyleAttribute("color",
"black");

 var ss = SpreadsheetApp.openById('0Aq1-C9Nl4dO-
dHRWNHd4d21IUHZjbnVlMktWZVY2Z3c').getSheets()[0];
 var range = ss.getRange(ss.getLastRow()+1, 1, 1, 2);

 var values = [[new Date(),e.parameter.textBox]];
 range.setValues(values);

 return app;
}
```

Verifying the Input

There are many ways to verify that you are getting an email address, but for our purpose, we will use the validators built into Google Script for filtering the input. This will ensure that what we get looks like an email address. There are ways to actually verify that the email address is an actual valid email, but that exceeds the scope of this chapter.

Along with the validation, you are also going to use client side handlers. There will be much more on this subject later in the book, but for now know that client side handlers run in the user's browser and are much faster than making an RPC to the server.

Validators prevent the handler from executing the function. This is a very simple modification where .validateEmail(*widget*) is added in the handler:

```
var handler = app.createServerHandler('contactMe')
    .validateEmail(email)
    .addCallbackElement(mainPanel);
button.addClickHandler(handler);
```

Or for the GUI Builder:

```
var handler = app.createServerClickHandler('contactMe')
        .addCallbackElement(app.getElementById('mainPanel'))
        .validateEmail(app.getElementById('textBox'));
app.getElementById('button').addClickHandler(handler);
```

Now entering anything that is not an email address will not be allowed to pass. However, from the user's perspective it will look like nothing is happening or that the button is not working. In addition to stopping the execution of the function if the input is incorrect, you also need to place some notifications on the screen to let the user know what is wrong.

Just above the handler you created in the doGet function, add a new client handler. This will run on the client's side and is very responsive.

Start out by building the handler:

```
var validateEmail = app.createClientHandler()
```

Now use the negated form of validate Email—validateNotEmail—which will run more methods if the validation finds a wrong value. What we want to do to notify the user is to set the email text to red and put a message in the info label about what is wrong.

Use forTargets(widget) to get each element and then make the needed changes. Here you see the completed validation handler:

```
var validateEmail = app.createClientHandler()
  .validateNotEmail(email)
  .forTargets(email).setStyleAttribute("color", "red")
  .forTargets(info).setVisible(true)
    .setText('That's not an email')
    .setStyleAttribute("color", "red");
button.addClickHandler(validateEmail)
```

Or for the GUI Builder:

```
var validateEmail = app.createClientHandler()
  .validateNotEmail(app.getElementById('textBox'))
  .forTargets(app.getElementById('textBox')).setStyleAttribute("color", "red")
  .forTargets(app.getElementById('info')).setVisible(true)
    .setText('That's not an email')
    .setStyleAttribute("color", "red");
app.getElementById('button').addClickHandler(validateEmail)
```

Give it a run and see what you get. Notice that after you enter a non-email address, you get the message "That's not an email," and if you try again with a real email address, the message is replaced with the "Thank you" message.

Now that the user interaction is done, we need to find a place to store the information. In "Storing the Values" on page 36, we will finish this project, make the boss happy, and start gathering data.

Storing the Values

I have saved the best for last, or maybe the easiest part, depending on how you might look at it. The app you have been building has all the features needed to interact with the user, but we are lacking the most important thing: a place to store the data and a way to get it there. Not to worry, Google has provided us with several options that should work for most applications.

Store in a Spreadsheet

If you have been following along, your script is living on a Google Site and you have been accessing it through the published URL. What we need to do now is write the visitor email address to a spreadsheet. First, we will need a spreadsheet, so please open Google Docs and make one. You can name it anything you like.

Setting Up the Spreadsheet

The top row of our spreadsheet will be the column names so we know what the data is. (Yes, it is obvious for such a small app, but you know how things can grow.) In column A1 (uppermost-left), name the column **Time Stamp**. Next, name B1 **Email**. See Figure 4-1.

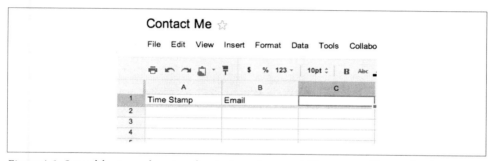

Figure 4-1. Spreadsheets can be set up for storing values much like one would use a database

Heading back to your script, you will need to add the code to open your new spreadsheet in the script so we can write the email value to it.

Above the line `return app;`, insert:

```
var ss = SpreadsheetApp.openById("<YourSpreadsheetIdGoesHere>").getSheets()[0];
```

Here we are creating a variable (ss) that will represent the first sheet in our spreadsheet. SpreadsheetsApp is a Google Script service, like UiApp. Having built-in services that we can call on in the same script makes using Google Script so easy. Next we will use the `openById` method to get the sheet we need to write data.

What is a Spreadsheet ID, you may be asking yourself? In Google Documents, everything including pictures, PDFs, presentations, and spreadsheets have a unique ID to keep track of them. Fortunately, it is also very easy to find. Select your spreadsheet and look in the address bar where the URL is.

You are looking for something like this:

```
key=0Aq1-C9Nl4dO-dHR4ZDFkV3FR4UDFFMXlrQXc&hl=en_US\
```

The key you need is between key= and &.

What you need to do is copy the ID and replace *<YourSpreadsheetIdGoesHere>*:

```
SpreadsheetApp.openById("0Aq1-C9Nl4dO-dHR4ZDFkV3FR4UDFFMXlrQXc")
```

The last part—.getSheets()[0]—simply gets the sheet furthest to the left, or the first one. Note that this is a zero-based call because .getSheets returns an array of the sheets in the spreadsheet. This is an application built to do just one thing and will only have one sheet, but if you are concerned that your sheet may move to be in a different place, it would be a good idea to use .getSheetByName(*name*). This way it doesn't matter where the sheet is just as long as the name stays the same.

It can be useful to know when a visitor submitted a request, so we will need to create a timestamp to go along with the email. When using Google Script, it's always good to look for ways to make your code more efficient. One of the best ways to do this is to minimize the number of calls you make to any of the other services, inside or outside of Google. While you can certainly write the data to a spreadsheet one cell at a time, you will likely run into timeout issues and it'll take forever.

The next thing we need to do is get the range of cells where we want to write our values. When accessing a spreadsheet you get the cells with the getRange method. There are several constructors for the method such as using 'A1' notation where the column letter and row number are used similarly to spreadsheet formulas, for example, ('A1') or ('A1:C6'). Letters can get confusing so there is also a constructor that accepts numbers in place of the column letters. We will use .getRange(*<row>*, *<column>*, *<numRows>*, *<numColumns>*):

```
    var range = ss.getRange(ss.getLastRow()+1, 1, 1, 2);
```

ss.getLastRow() returns the number of the last row of data. We want to write our new submission to the row after that, so we simply add one (+1). Next, we want to start a column, so *<column>* is represented by a 1. There is only one row of data to write, but with the date, it is going to be two columns wide, hence the 1 and 2 at the end of the set.

 When converting columns from letters to numbers, the first column is number one, A=1. However, after you get the values, they will be in a JavaScript array that is zero-based, meaning column A is now zero, not one.

Setting Up the Data

The data will need to be placed in what is known as a 2D array so that we only need to write to the spreadsheet once. Here is how that looks: [[row1 column1, row1 column2] , [row2 column1, row2 column2]], and so on as shown in Figure 4-2. Any amount of consecutive rows and columns can be written simultaneously in this way:

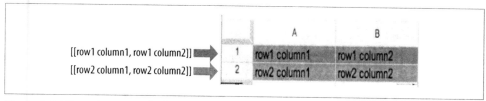

Figure 4-2. The getRange method creates a 2D array

Because we only have one row, the data looks like this:

```
var values = [[new Date(), e.parameter.textBox]];
```

Now that we have the range of cells and the data in a matching configuration, all that is left is to write it:

```
range.setValues(values);
```

Save your work and load up the web UI. Remember that you need to use an email address in the form or the validation trigger. After pressing the Sign Up button, you should receive a "Thank you" message and the email address in the form will be reset to a blank text box. In the spreadsheet, you will see the results of all your hard work over the last two chapters. See Figure 4-3. Please refer to Chapter 1 for a refresher on placing the UI as a gadget in your site.

Figure 4-3. Each entry is saved in the spreadsheet and timestamped.

Final code for the UiApp style:

```
function doGet() {
  var app = UiApp.createApplication();

  app.add(app.loadComponent("MyGui"));

  //Validation
    var validateEmail = app.createClientHandler()
      .validateNotEmail(app.getElementById('textBox'))
      .forTargets(app.getElementById('textBox')).setStyleAttribute("color", "red")
      .forTargets(app.getElementById('info')).setVisible(true)
        .setText('Please enter a valid email address')
        .setStyleAttribute("color", "red");
    app.getElementById('button').addClickHandler(validateEmail);
```

```
//handler
var handler = app.createServerClickHandler('contactMe')
        .addCallbackElement(app.getElementById('mainPanel'))
        .validateEmail(app.getElementById('textBox'));
app.getElementById('button').addClickHandler(handler);

return app;
}

function contactMe(e){
 var app = UiApp.getActiveApplication();

 app.getElementById('textBox').setValue('').setStyleAttribute("color", "black");
 app.getElementById('info').setText('Thank you!').setStyleAttribute("color",
"black");

 var ss = SpreadsheetApp.openById('0Aq1-C9Nl4dO-
dHRWNHd4d21IUHZjbnVlMktWZVY2Z3c').getSheets()[0];
 var range = ss.getRange(ss.getLastRow()+1, 1, 1, 2);

 var values = [[new Date(),e.parameter.textBox]];
 range.setValues(values);

 return app;
}
```

Final code for the handcoded style:

```
function doGet() {
  var app = UiApp.createApplication();

  var mainPanel = app.createVerticalPanel().setId('mainPanel');
  app.add(mainPanel);

  mainPanel.add(app.createLabel('Enter your email to sign up'));

  var form = app.createHorizontalPanel();
  mainPanel.add(form);

  var email = app.createTextBox().setName('textBox').setId('textBox');
  form.add(email);

  var button = app.createButton('Sign up');
  form.add(button);

  var info = app.createLabel().setVisible(false).setId('info');
  mainPanel.add(info);

  //Validation
    var validateEmail = app.createClientHandler()
      .validateNotEmail(email)
      .forTargets(email).setStyleAttribute("color", "red")
      .forTargets(info).setVisible(true)
        .setText('Please enter a valid email address')
        .setStyleAttribute("color", "red");
```

```
    button.addClickHandler(validateEmail)

  //handler
  var handler = app.createServerHandler('contactMe')
      .validateEmail(email)
      .addCallbackElement(mainPanel);
  button.addClickHandler(handler);

  return app;
}

function contactMe(e){
 var app = UiApp.getActiveApplication();

 app.getElementById('textBox').setValue('').setStyleAttribute("color", "black");
 app.getElementById('info').setText('Thank you!').setStyleAttribute("color",
"black");

 var ss = SpreadsheetApp.openById('0Aq1-C9Nl4dO-
dHRWNHd4d21IUHZjbnVlMktWZVY2Z3c').getSheets()[0];
 var range = ss.getRange(ss.getLastRow()+1, 1, 1, 2);

 var values = [[new Date(),e.parameter.textBox]];
 range.setValues(values);

 return app;
}
```

PART II

Building Enterprise Applications

CHAPTER 5

Dynamic Details Using CSS

Monday morning, finishing your last drops of coffee, you begin contemplating how there always seems to be a direct relationship between the Power button on a computer and resolved help desk service tickets. Suddenly, Frank, the middle manager with a propensity for last minute drama about any project requiring more than a paper clip, bursts into your cubical, breathless and ranting. Between his wheezing, you discern that there is a problem with the new product information pages. "Too wordy, too cluttered, and too darn difficult to understand" are the sharper points of his reproach. Most of all, "the others"—his euphemism meaning the rest of the sales world—have fantastic looking pages. "How could we have let this slide and why didn't we see it coming?" he laments. With a few gentle words, you calm Frank to a point of incoherent babbling and send him back to his office with a promise that you will do something to fight off those meanies and save the company from utter destruction.

Fighting Clutter

As more and more information is added to a web page, it becomes a jumble of images and text that flow together, losing the reader in a jungle of clutter where they slash away with their mouse pointers in an attempt to find that one key artifact. We all want to keep the customers coming back for more, and that requires us to ensure they have a great experience when visiting our site. While we want to provide an abundance of information to persuade the customer that he is dealing with a knowledgeable dealer, too much information can cause the customer to not find what he is seeking.

Customers are visual browsers when it comes to choosing products. After all, a catalog is worthless without pictures of products; and your website is an online catalog. Often the better visual presentation you make of a product, the more sales it will generate. A good way to gauge what you present to customers is by comparing it with big media providers like Netflix and YouTube. These mega retailers have discovered that they can pack more items on a web page by moving the description and purchasing mechanism to a pop-up panel, thus gaining more product impressions per pageview. Figure 5-1 shows an example of displaying six items where a traditional web page would only have room for two.

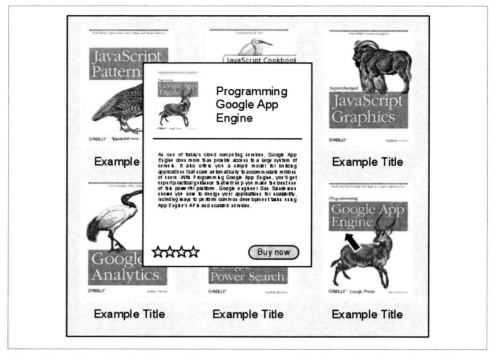

Figure 5-1. This optimized web page shows more content to the viewer than the traditional layout.

When shopping the Web, we naturally look for the picture of an item first; it's likely hardwired into our hunter gatherer genes to do so. For example, have you ever began a web search for "beautiful sunset pictures" by reading descriptions about sunsets? No, you go to the images straight away. I know you also read reviews about products, but if something strikes your fancy, your next thought is most likely, "What does it look like?" Displaying more items on a page becomes very important to the user's experience, and that is what this chapter is all about. As you work through this chapter, keep in mind that there are three major components: the image repository, the database, and the products gadget, which is embedded into the Google Site.

What You Will Learn

You will learn how to:

- Use script gadgets in Google Sites
- Work with CSS

- Dynamically add elements to a flex table
- Work with the Google Sites service
- Build powerful visual effects
- Create JavaScript data objects
- Use public classes

Supplies

You will need:

- A Google Site
- Product images
- Product descriptions

Application Overview

Your task here is to help Frank keep his sanity by building an application that can be embedded into the company's Google Site and maximize page space, showing as many products as possible to the customer while supplying them the information they need to make a wise purchase.

Image File Repository

There are as many ways to keep a product list as there are websites listing products, so if you already have your system in place, you will need to do some research on how web service–friendly it is. Google Script gives you the ability to connect to databases, SOAP, and WSDL services, like the Amazon Web Services Client, JSON, and all of the Google API services. To keep things simple and get you developing right away, we will use all Google services to set up your products page.

Load up your Google Site or create a new one, and create a new file cabinet page called Products. Figure 5-2 shows an example of the Products image repository. This is where you will store the image files for each product, so get busy with the "Add file" button.

Keep in mind that we will be setting the dimensions of the images in the UI, but it is a good idea to have your product images close to the same dimensions, and the same dimensions of the largest settings you will use to display it. This way you can avoid ugly pixelated images that will cause your boss to fume and customers to avert their eyes in disgust. You don't need to add a description here in the image repository, but it can be helpful when identifying what you are working with months from now.

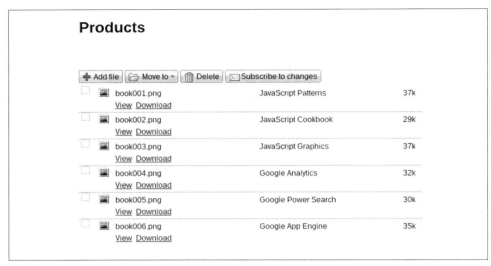

Figure 5-2. File cabinet pages are a convenient way to store files on the Web.

Setting Up the Database

Whether you are a web designer by trade or the designated IT geek in the office, you are likely too busy to keep up with and maintain every aspect of the company's website. In the past, it took a webmaster, and her secret ways, to make every change required to keep the website current. In the fast changing web of today, that is simply more work than any one person should be tasked with. What if you get sick or go on vacation? Will you teach someone to hardcode each product into the website? Heck no, and this is why you need a database that is easy for staff to understand, simple to update, and able to automatically roll out changes to the website. Surprisingly, a spreadsheet is an excellent choice for this task because there is little to no training required to use it.

There are four main product elements you need to share with your customers: the image, the title, the description, and the link to more information. Certainly more information like customer ratings, similar products, and category information are also excellent options to consider, and I encourage you to add them; you will have the skills for that soon.

Open a new spreadsheet and name it **Product Database**. Name the columns **ID**, **Title**, **Description**, **Image URL**, and **Product Page** as shown in Figure 5-3.

You now have an image repository and a database. Next you will make entries in the database that represent each product.

Loading the Database

A very good reason for using a spreadsheet for your database is because they are familiar to most office workers, which means you can delegate maintaining the products page

Project Database ☆

File　Edit　View　Insert　Format　Data　Tools　Collaborate　Help　　Saved seconds ago

	A	B	C	D	E
1	ID	Title	Description	Image URL	Product Page
2					
3					
4					
5					
6					
7					
8					
9					
10					

Figure 5-3. Spreadsheet set up as a database for the image repository

to anyone, even people outside of IT like sales. A spreadsheet is easy to use and in the case of a Google spreadsheet, you will be able to update the website from anywhere, including your cell phone. This brings me to another point: there is a two-step process going on here, where pictures are loaded to a Site and then the spreadsheet is updated. I have set it up this way to keep the content of this chapter at a reasonable level, but later on in the book you will learn techniques for building a UI that uploads files and allows for describing them, essentially, reducing the two steps here in this chapter to one.

The ID column is the product's unique identifier, meaning the same number should never appear more than once in that column.

Never start the ID with a number or include special characters or spaces. Later you will use the ID for each row to name JavaScript objects and that means they must be JavaScript safe variable names.

The order of the numbering is not important in this column, just that they are unique numbers for each row so the correct item can be later selected.

This handy function will help you create random numbers in the "A" column of your Product Database spreadsheet after you have filled out the other columns:

```
function randomString() {
  var ss = SpreadsheetApp.getActiveSheet();
  var randomArray = new Array();
  var chars = "ABCDEFGHIJKLMNOPQRSTUVWXTZabcdefghiklmnopqrstuvwxyz";
  var string_length = 10;
  var lastRow = ss.getLastRow()-1;
  for (var j=0; j<lastRow; j++){
    var randomstring = '';
    for (var i=0; i<string_length; i++) {
      var rnum = Math.floor(Math.random() * chars.length);
      randomstring += chars.substring(rnum,rnum+1);
    }
}
```

```
      randomArray.push([randomstring]);
    }
    ss.getRange(2, 1, lastRow, 1).setValues(randomArray);
  }
```

This function will not check to see if the IDs generated are unique, but the odds of coming up with the same ID in a ten character string taken from 52 choices is, well, let's just say if you do get a duplicate, go buy a lottery ticket now.

If you are completely paranoid about ensuring you have truly unique values, insert a temporary column to the left of "A" and insert this formula in cell "A1": =unique(B2:B*your last row number*) if you have the same total row values in column "A" as in column "B" they are all unique. Delete the temporary column "A".

Next, the Title column will be the name of the product. It should be short, one word if possible, so that it fits well in our scheme. The Title will appear in two places in the UI: once under the image and again in the pop-up information panel. The size of the text will be much different for each instance of the Title and that will be accomplished using CSS.

For the description, you will want a paragraph that is concise and provides just enough information for the customer to decide if this is the product they are looking for or if they should continue looking. One of the problems with the traditional web page is that each time you click a product, you are taken to a different page. Depending on connection speed, this can get monotonous and frustrate customers by having to constantly move up to the back arrow immediately after making a selection. The effect you are seeking will use mouse overs to show and hide each product. This approach allows the customer to quickly zero in on the specific item they are looking for and allows you to reap the benefits of their happy return to find more merchandise.

The simplest way to get the Image URL is by right-clicking on the view link in the repository and selecting "Copy link address." At the end of the URL you may see ? attredirects=0. This can be removed or left alone, as it will not affect the outcome.

The last column of this example is the product page, and it is a URL that will take the user to more information, an opportunity to make a purchase, or both. There are several ways the product link can be used. For example, the mouse over image on the product listing page could use this link if the customer is certain she wants that item and would like to go directly to its page; a button on the pop-up panel gives them a second opportunity to click through. You will create these pages in the next section.

Creating Pages from a Spreadsheet

You have your Unique IDs generated, titles, descriptions, and Image URLs entered into the Products Database spreadsheet. Now it is time to create all those individual web pages where the customer will go when she wants all the juicy details. You could begin the laborious process of creating each page one at a time from the Sites Management service, but what if you have 100 or more products? This would take days of tedious, repetitive work to complete. Wait a minute, Google Script is built to automate Google products. Next you will learn how to use Google Script to create web pages and fill them with HTML content from a spreadsheet.

Using the Public Google Script Objects Class

There are some tasks in Google Script, like creating an object from a range of data in a spreadsheet, that use the same code regardless of the application you are writing. This is where open source libraries can be very handy. If you have done any JavaScript programming, you are likely familiar with jQuery, one of the most popular open source libraries for that language.

 Google Script is a young language and there are not many references out there. In writing this book, the author felt it would be helpful to shorten your production time by creating several "Foundation classes" to take care of the minutia of coding common tasks. Having common generic open source code in one place is what makes languages great. You can find information about these open source classes on the Script Examples (*http://sites.google.com/site/scriptsexamples/custom-methods/*) website and the source code at O'Reilly.

In JavaScript, a library is typically saved as a .js file on your server and loaded using:

```
<script src="jquery.js"></script>
```

Because Google Script is cloud-based, you will need to store open source libraries in your script project. This means you will be storing the library code on Google's servers instead of your own. There is a lot of discussion about allowing the importing of public libraries directly into Google Script by calling on a URL or script ID. This could certainly reduce the code you have in your script, but it may open your application to security issues. Open source code is also updated regularly, which could induce a broken state in your application. The best practice at this time is to copy the source into your script and inspect it before use.

These open source libraries can be large, and you don't what to sift through all that code to see what you are working on. Therefore, keeping open source libraries organized is key in managing large applications.

Installing an Open Source Library

Start by creating a new script in the Product Database spreadsheet.

Click File, and select New➡File.

In the "Create file" window, type **GS Objects**.

This creates a new file in your script where you should copy and paste the open source library code (See Figure 5-4). Unlike the file system on a web server, the files in your script project do not require a reference, such as /utilities.js, when writing the code. Everything in every file is available everywhere in the script.

 When writing your applications, be careful that you don't duplicate variable and other code element names within different files. Duplication will not throw an error, but it will certainly give you unexpected results.

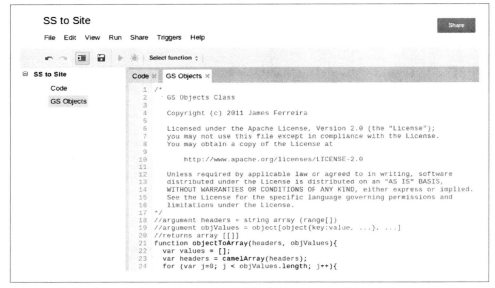

Figure 5-4. The files makes it easy to manage and update open source libraries.

Create Pages and Fill the Spreadsheet

Creating a Google Sites page from Google Script is easy because of the built-in Sites Services (*http://code.google.com/googleapps/appsscript/service_sites.html*) that gives you access to create and change every aspect of a Site. Automatically updating content, changing permissions, and pushing up new pages from custom templates that you design in the Sites manager are possible using Sites Services.

To get your product pages automatically built, we will use a generic web page template, but if you are working off a site that is already built, feel free to look at the documentation and add the pages using a custom template.

```
var site = SitesApp.getSiteByUrl('Your Site URL');
```

The method (*http://code.google.com/googleapps/appsscript/class_page.html#createWeb Page*), `createWebPage(title, name, html)`, is what you use to create pages in a Site. The `title` argument is what you will see at the top of the page and in the navigation links. Don't confuse `title` with `name`, which is the page URL name. In the Products Database there is a column named "Title", which is what we want to display on our pages and in this simple use case, the URL might as well match the title. This may be fine depending on the titles you use, but spaces and special characters are not going to work well in a page URL, and the Script Editor will complain about invalid page names if you try to run it like that. Here is where the GS Objects class `camelString(String)` method will help.

Throughout this book you will be pulling column headers, widget names, and IDs into your script. To make these work, they will need to be JavaScript safe or more commonly referred to as camelCase (*http://en.wikipedia.org/wiki/Camel_text*). This means removing spaces, special characters, numbers at the beginning, and anything else that JavaScript might find obnoxious. To convert a string over to camelCase use:

```
camelString('Title');
```

Now you have the title, name, and description arguments properly formatted and ready to create pages by iterating through your rows of data in the spreadsheet. Well, sort of, but there is one more problem: when you call `getRange` on a spreadsheet it will bring the data back just as it appeared in the spreadsheet, but in an array `[[ID, Title, Description, Image URL, Product Page], [aLHeBRCUtT, JavaScript Patterns, Now...]]`. This way you can call out values as you would in any array.

 Spreadsheets start with "1", but arrays in your script are zero-based, meaning they start with zero. For example, consider `rangeArray[row][column]`. To get the value for row 2, column 2, you would write: `rangeArray[1][1]`.

To get the Title from column B, count A=0, B=1. This is fine in a very short script when you will be the only user, but let's say a friendly coworker comes along and rearranges your columns. The problem here is that making an Enterprise application means it will be used everyday and by many different people. You need to plan for some user created issues. Furthermore, sooner or later you will run into an application that has columns CD, CE, etc. and out comes the calculator, 26*2+4... The headache continues. To solve this problem and keep your script from breaking, you need a way to get the values by asking for them by name and not the ambiguous column they are in.

JavaScript objects are something that takes time to get your head around, but don't worry, the GS Objects class will do the work, allowing you to use the objects without the fuss of figuring out how to create them. Here is how it works: get the data range that you want from the spreadsheet and use `rangeToObjects(range)` on the resulting array:

```
var ss = SpreadsheetApp.getActiveSheet();
var productDetails = rangeToObjects(ss.getDataRange().getValues());
```

Now what you have is an array of JavaScript objects that looks like this: [{id=aLHeBR CUtT, title=JavaScript Patterns, …},{...}] Each element in the array is an object with property names made from the column headers (camelCase of course) that contain the values from each column. If you would like to get the Title of the item in the third spreadsheet row use:

```
productDetails[1].title    //don't forget arrays are zero based
```

Keep in mind that the array is zero-based and that you are starting with the data rows excluding the headers that are in row one. See Figure 5-5. Spreadsheet Row 1=headers, Row 2=first data row. Therefore, `productDetails[0]` is the first row of data.

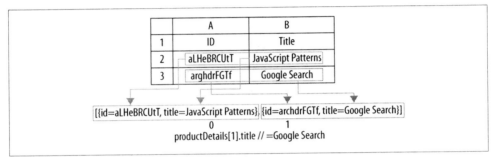

Figure 5-5. toDataObjects returns an array of row objects

Not only is this much easier to understand, it also solves the problems of moving columns around and counting up the alphabet. Don't forget that the object property representing the column header is in camelCase. If you are having problems figuring out what your column name has turned into, just run it through the `camelString("1 Test Value")`.

To create the pages, you will iterate through the `productDetails` object and build each page row by row. We have covered the `title` and the page URL (`name`) arguments of the `createWebPage` method on page 53, but there is also the opportunity to create the page content in the `html` argument. Because these are products and you have already stored the image, why not get a big head start on the detailed pages by automatically inserting the image and description text? If you use an additional "page template" argument, elements like purchasing, advertising, and other aspects could be applied giving you a finished presentation in this step. Save that for your homework; for now we will focus on the basics of creating a default web page and adding the content we have in the Product Database.

When writing the HTML page content, only focus on what would normally be inside the `<body></body>` tag. It is possible to add a variety of content this way but with some limitations on scripting processes, which Google will kindly strip out. A script using an HTML template containing replaceable keys could achieve very complex effects. For the product pages you will use a very basic template that is built into the script and adds the image tags and description.

Following is the for loop that creates the pages:

```
for (var i=0; i<productDetails.length; i++){
    var page = site.createWebPage(productDetails[i].title,
                        camelString(productDetails[i].title),
                        '<img src="'+productDetails[i].imageUrl+
                        '" align="left"/><p>'+productDetails[i].description);
    productDetails[i].productPage = page.getUrl();
}
```

The `productDetails` array contains an entry representing each row in the data range. You iterate it by getting its length.

Next, create a variable `page` that will represent the web page returned by calling `site.createWebPage`. You could simply call on the Sites Service directly without a variable, but the database needs to know the page URL for each product and you get that from the returned page object. The arguments are filled in as discussed using the `pro ductDetails[i].column header`.

The last line in the for loop works opposite the others and sets the page URL value into `productDetails[i].productPage`. This means that the `productDetails` object now contains new information that will need to be written back to the spreadsheet after the loop completes.

 Why not write to the spreadsheet in the loop? Keep in mind that an RPC callback has to execute every time you write to the spreadsheet. Depending on how much data you have and the number of writes, this could take a very long time and from the user's point of view it may appear that the application has become unresponsive. Always limit or group calls together for better performance.

The last step in the script will write the changed values back to the Products Database. Start by getting the headers; you never know, they might have changed in the last few milliseconds. In the next line, use the method `objToArray` from the GS Objects class to turn your `productDetails` object back into a spreadsheet range array:

```
var headers = ss.getRange(1,1,1,ss.getLastColumn()).getValues()[0];
var values = objectToArray(headers, productDetails);
ss.getRange(2, 1, values.length, values[0].length).setValues(values);
```

All that's left to do is write the values back to the spreadsheet. Because you used the spreadsheet headers to recreate the values, everything will line up in the correct column.

Save and run the script. You will see that the page URLs have filled in and clicking one will open the product page complete with an image and description, as shown in Figure 5-6.

Figure 5-6. Automating page creation can save hours of time.

Half a chapter later and you don't have a UI yet. Hang in there; before you can build a castle you need a solid foundation and that is what you have built. The image repository, database, and product pages are ready to feed into the UI, which is where we are going next.

Creating the Products UI

One feature of the Products UI is that items can be added or removed from the database without needing to recode any of the components. Simply, reloading the web page will cause the UI to reflect the changes. This makes it possible for you, the developer, to step away allowing less technical people to perform the data entry.

The script you built earlier to create pages can handle figuring out which pages are already done to avoid making a duplicate. Add an `if` statement just inside the `for` loop to check "empty" value in the "Product Page" column.

```
if (productDetails[i].productPage != "")
    continue;
```

The `continue` will simply skip to the next round in the loop if any value is found.

By controlling spreadsheet permissions, you create a system for managing the content on your site but in a way that anyone can understand with little or no training.

When beginning to develop a complex UI it is helpful to break it down into smaller parts and build them one at a time. This modular approach is also helpful when you need to upgrade parts of the code. Breaking down this UI, there are product images to display with a certain number across the page and in rows continuing down. The title will go under each image and link to the product page. The next part happens when the mouse passes over the image. This will require a few handlers: the one to display more information and the other to hide the information when the mouse moves away from the image. You need something to display, therefore building an information panel will be the next part. Finally, it will take CSS to get the whole page looking good and your information panel hovering over the other content.

Displaying Products

For this section, the script will be written in the Sites Script Editor allowing you to easily insert the UI as a gadget in any page.

Open your Products Site and create a new script.

As you work through the development steps, it is much easier to preview the UI using the standalone page. Enter in the basic UiApp elements for the doGet(e) function and publish the UiApp. When you load the published URL, there won't be anything to look at, but you will also know that everything is working if there are no errors and the title of your application is displayed in the tab info:

```
function doGet(e) {
  var application = UiApp.createApplication().setTitle('Products UI');
  //Your App
  return application;
}
```

Products will be listed in rows down the page, and you may not know how many products are going to be in the database at any given time. The Flex Table widget is the appropriate choice for this task. It works exactly like a Grid but does not require pre-defining the size.

Why not a panel? In this case you want each product to be in a cell of its own, making it easy to keep everything lined up on the page and control spacing around them. Unless you know for certain that a grid will always remain the same size, use a Flex Table.

Create the productsTable and set its cell padding to 20:

```
var productsTable = app.createFlexTable().setCellPadding(20);
app.add(productsTable);
```

When the images go in, they will need some space around them. This will ensure a good appearance and also help the mouse over handlers to not get confused.

The bigger picture of the application is that it only contains two parent elements: the productsTable for holding images of the products and an info panel that pops up over the top. There will be all kinds of complexity within these large structures, but it will help to think of your code in chunks as shown in Figure 5-7.

In the UiApp, each added item goes to the bottom of the page, however, the element at the bottom of the page is actually on the top of the stack because it was the last item

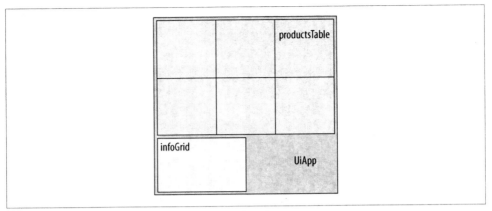

Figure 5-7. The two parent widgets displayed within the UiApp

added. When you start using CSS to free the different elements from inlining, they will cover each other on the page. Because the infoGrid needs to float over the products table, it will be the last item added to the UiApp.

You might be wondering about the infoGrid, and you are correct in guessing that it is a grid. Here is its construction:

```
var infoGrid = app.createGrid(1,1).setId('infoGrid').setVisible(false);
app.add(infoGrid);
```

First note that it is a single-celled grid. Many of the widgets in the UiApp can hold other widgets within them. For example, the single cell of the infoGrid could hold a panel with hundreds of elements inside or nested in it. Having such an element gives you a target to build more complex UIs. We will go into more detail on why this is important later in "Adding Action" on page 61.

Another aspect of the infoGrid: it is invisible or rather set to visible `false`. When an element is not visible, you can't see it, but also note that it will not take up space on the page. This is also true for the Hidden type of widget.

Get the Products

The products are loaded into an object using the method in "Create Pages and Fill the Spreadsheet" on page 52. The only difference is the `openById` method from the `SpreadsheetApp`. Whenever your script needs to access a spreadsheet remotely, meaning it is not built into the spreadsheet, you open it by its unique ID. The ID of all the Google Docs products is a long string of random characters between the `key=` and `&hl` tags in the URL. For example:

https://docs.google.com/a/ex.com/spreadsheet/ccc?key=<*LongLONG string*>&hl=en_US#gid=0

```
var ss = SpreadsheetApp.openById('YourDocumentKey').getSheets()[0];
var range = ss.getDataRange().getValues();
var productDetails = rangeToObjects(range);
```

Notice that we are being very specific here with the spreadsheet by ID and the sheet we want by using `.getSheets()[0]`. Again, we see a zero-based array returned as the sheets in this spreadsheet. This certain array starts with the leftmost sheet and counts right.

 Someone might want to move your sheets around and that will break your script. If you feel this might happen, name the sheet and use `.getSheetByName(name)` in place of `.getSheets()[0]`. You will still need to tell people not to change the name so it is a toss up of what will be most effective.

Load the UI

Now that you have all the data loaded in our handy `productDetails` object, it is time to iterate through it and create the widgets for display. Before we get too carried away —I know you can't wait to show the boss something—some thought needs to be given to the layout of the products. In Figure 5-1, there are three products across the page and two rows for a total of six. Simply iterating the array and putting items in the Flex Table gives us a list, which is what we don't want.

For now, add in a few variables to represent rows and columns, and they will be explained throughout the loop:

```
var r = 0;
var c = 0;
```

Each product has two elements, the image and the title. They are stacked vertically. Keep in mind that they will be added to the `infoTable`, but they need to stay together and act as one widget in a single cell, not two objects in two cells. To accomplish this, create a vertical panel and place both items inside. Here is the full loop as reference while each line is explained:

```
for (var i in productDetails){
  var image = app.createImage(productDetails[i].imageUrl)
      .setHeight('300px')
      .setId(productDetails[i].id); //handlers will go here
  var title = app.createAnchor(productDetails[i].title,
productDetails[i].productPage);

  var productPanel = app.createVerticalPanel();
  productPanel.add(image);
  productPanel.add(title);

  productsTable.setWidget(r, c, productPanel);
  c++
  if (c == 3){
    c = 0;
    r++;
```

```
    }
    //save spot for CSS
}
```

Using the for loop, var in array makes for a clean way to iterate these products. When you see the "i" referred to, as in [i], that is a whole row from the spreadsheet.

The first element is the image and it is created from the value in productDe tails[i].imageUrl. It is a good idea to control the size of the image because you never know what you might get. Good preparation of the images, like sizing, is always best to do before they go into the repository. Here the height is set but the width is not. Sizing both can create some artistic effects that might not go over well with the PR department, so use your best judgment.

If you think back to Chapter 1, everything you want to reference in the UiApp must have an ID, name, or both. Set the ID of the image to be the ID of the product using productDetails[i].id. Later, when we wire up the handlers and mouse functions, the ID of the image will tell us which item needs to be retrieved from the database.

Moving on to the title, note that it is a hyperlink also known as an Anchor tag, <a>, when writing in HTML. Using the title as an anchor will give the user a way to click and open the product's page in a new window. To create the title link, we use the createAnchor method, which has the arguments ("Link Text", URL). You get the argument values from the productDetails object using productDetails[i].title and productDetails[i].productPage.

Now that you have created an image and the link to the product, you want them to appear stacked together on the page. This is done by adding both elements to a vertical panel, which we will name productPanel. Because this panel is inside the for loop, it is recreated as a new object on each iteration so its variable can be the same without causing a problem.

Next, this product [i] needs to be loaded into the productsTable, but where? To nest a widget within another, use the setWidget method and the appropriate arguments. For example, the variables created earlier–r for row and c for column—plug into product sTable along with the productPanel, forming a complete statement:

```
    productsTable.setWidget(r, c, productPanel);
```

Because r and c were instantiated with the value 0, this iteration of product panel will be added to the top left cell in the productsTable. Each time the for loop iterates, new copies of the image, title, and product panel are made. The values change because [i] has changed. The way to distinguish them is by setting an ID, as was done by using the ID value of each product provided from the spreadsheet.

The products look right with three across the page, so this will take a new counter within the loop that iterates the total number of products. Unlike the variables created inside the loop such as the image, that are recreated on each iteration, r and c are outside the loop and will hold their value from one iteration to the next.

After loading the first product into the `productsTable`, use `c++` to increment by 1. The next iteration will have `c=1` and `r=0`, allowing the next product to be loaded one cell right in the `productsTable` but in the same row. An `if` statement will check to see if `c` has reached 3, the total number of columns we want to go across the page, and if so, reset `c` to 0 and increment `r`. This will continue until there are no more items in `productDetails`. It really does not matter if there are 2, 6, or 365 products in the spreadsheet. There will be three across, and the total divided by three rows. Because the ID of each item was set, an item can be anywhere in the Flex Table, but finding it is not a problem.

Save your work and load the published URL in your browser; your products will magically jump into place. At this point you have a typical database-driven products page common on the Web. Each product has a link under it to take the user to a new page with more details; closing that page brings the user back to the list page. The rest of this chapter will focus on bringing life into this page by making it interactive.

Adding Action

Creating action in the UiApp requires two components: a handler attached to a widget and a function outside of `doGet`, which the handler will execute. There are several handler types: click handlers for buttons and links; key press handlers, which are useful in detecting the Enter key in a text box; and mouse handlers that will run when the mouse moves over or off of your element. There are several more handlers; for this application, the mouse over and mouse out are used.

When creating a handler it takes the argument `function` in quotes. In this application there will be two functions, one to show the `infoPanel` and another to hide it. Because each handler can only fire one function, you will need to create two handlers.

In order for a handler to change an element in the UI, it needs to have a callback element so the server knows where to send the information. This is done using the `addCallback Element` method and the object that you plan to change. If you will be changing many items on the page, they all need to have the same parent and you'll pass the parent in the callback. For example, a main panel may have labels, buttons, and grids added to it. When you pass the main panel in the callback, all the widgets become available. Sending everything every time is more data and could cause performance problems, so you will have to balance that. Here we only need to send the infoGrid.

Add the following code to the image widget:

```
.addMouseOverHandler(app.createServerMouseHandler('onInfo_')
.addCallbackElement(infoGrid))
.addMouseOutHandler(app.createServerMouseHandler('offInfo_')
.addCallbackElement(infoGrid));
```

The first part is to add the mouse over handler to the image. I know that sounds backwards but stay with me. Inside the `addMouseOverHandler` argument is where you create the handler that will fire the `onInfo_` function each time the mouse rolls over the image.

You can then add a callback directly to the new handler. Mind the closing) for the `addMouseOverHandler(` and then repeat with a mouse out handler `addMouseOutHandler`, which will execute the `offInfo_` function.

> You may see many examples of creating a variable for a handler like this:
>
> `var handler = app.createServerMouseHandler('function')`
>
> This will work in most cases but becomes unstable when creating many handlers in a table as done in this chapter. Instead add them directly to the widget.

Outside of the `doGet(){}` function brackets, create two new functions:

```
function offInfo(e){
  //code goes here
}

function onInfo(e){
  //code goes here
}
```

The `offInfo` function is very simple, it will get the `infoGrid` and set its visibility to false whenever the mouse moves off the image. Whenever you are executing a function from a handler that also calls back, it must load the active application and return it.

```
var application = UiApp.getActiveApplication();
app.getElementById('infoGrid').setVisible(false);
return application;
```

> There are a few points to make when using `app.getElementById('name')`. Always use with `UiApp.getActiveApplication()` in functions remote from the function where `UiApp.createApplication` was used. In the function where the UiApp was created call on the elements directly by their variable name, unless the elements were created using the GUI builder. In the GUI Builder case use `app.getElementById('name')`

Build the Information Panel

It seems like a drum roll would be a good opening to this section where you will add the final functionality to the application. Interestingly, the `onInfo` function bears a striking resemblance to `doGet`. This is because many of the same things need to happen. For starters the information from the database will need to be loaded into an object and iterated in order to search for the one that has been moused over. Then information will be loaded into a panel much in the way each image was inserted into the `program sTable`.

Create and load a `productDetails` object as demonstrated in "Get the Products" on page 58. To find and display the correct information we need to know which image was moused over. When creating the new functions I hope you noticed the e argument. e contains the values sent from the handler and a few extras. e.parameter.source is a special parameter that contains the ID of the item for which the handler was added. This element is often referred to as the caller. In this case the caller is the image and each one was named by the ID for its product. Now that was handy.

```
var id = e.parameter.source;
```

To load the correct product you will iterate through productDetails and check if there is a match for the ID. If the IDs match load up the product.

```
for (var i in  productDetails){
    if(productDetails[i].id == id){
```

The intent of the info panel is to provide more information about the product. This might include size, color, rating or other information. In the database there is a description for each object so that will be the additional information used in this example. Starting with a drawing like Figure 5-8 is a great way to mock up the elements needed to create a UI.

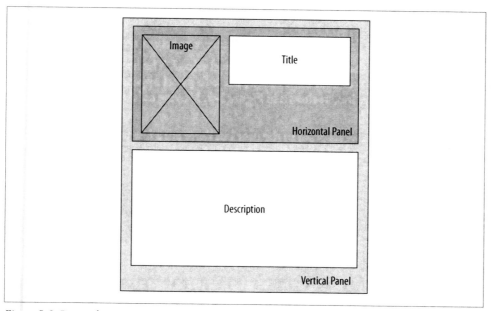

Figure 5-8. Remember to pay attention to how things are layered. The objects on the bottom get added to the UI first.

The image and title are next to each other so they go in a horizontal panel. The description will go below therefore, place the horizontal panel followed by the description in a vertical panel.

Because the loop was stopped when the ID was found [i] is the correct location for the product. Load the values to the correct locations and don't forget that the database columns are cameled.

```
var infoPanel = app.createVerticalPanel().setSize('300px', '300px');
var horzPanel = app.createHorizontalPanel();
var image = app.createImage(productDetails[i].imageUrl).setHeight('150px');
var title = app.createLabel(productDetails[i].title);
horzPanel.add(image);
horzPanel.add(title);
var description = app.createLabel(productDetails[i].description);
infoPanel.add(horzPanel);
infoPanel.add(description);
```

Now that the infoPanel is done and contains the correct product information it gets set into the infoGrid back in the doGet function. This is a good example of building a complex UI within a single cell of a grid. break stops the loop because the panel is loaded and iterating the rest of the list would waste time.

```
app.getElementById('infoGrid').setVisible(true)
    .setWidget(0,0, infoPanel);
break;
    }
}
```

That is the end of the functionality, but don't forget to return the application.

Save your work, find the UIs published page, and reload. The images load as expected but now when you hover over each image, the info panel appears at the bottom with the additional information, as shown in Figure 5-9. Moving off the image hides the info panel.

The application will now respond to the user but there are a few issues left to deal with. In the next section, you will learn about using CSS to place the panel where you want it and dress up the whole UI.

Styled with CSS

You're getting close to finishing and that's a good thing because Frank was spotted not long ago, out of his office and coming this way. While you have the interaction working, the info panel is in the wrong place and the page lacks style.

CSS has taken over style on the web and why not use it here as well. The main benefit to CSS is that it can be stored in a separate file and changed to create a totally different look without going into the code. In Google Script, CSS is applied at the widget level using the setStyleAttribute(name, value) method. This is problematic because not only do you need to apply CSS to each widget, you have to apply each style individually. To add insult to injury, style is not applied globally meaning making changes throughout the code just to accomplish a simple task like changing font size.

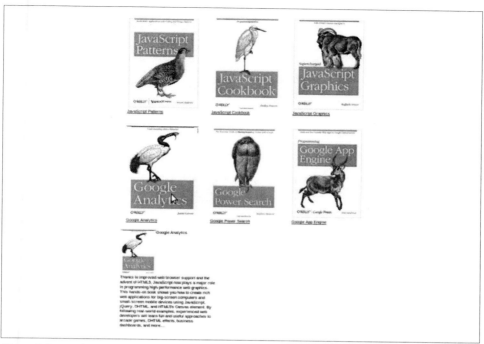

Figure 5-9. It's alive! The Application has become interactive.

This just won't do, CSS should work like well, CSS. To make CSS an easy to use option several components are added to the script:

- CSS file
- function to process CSS
- CSS "tags" applied to elements

In the editor, create a new file named CSS. This will work like the CSS files you have seen for HTML but contained withing the script. To stay consistent with the schema commonly in use on the web your CSS will be written the same with one exception, each style pair is separated with a colon not a comma.

The CSS file contains the following:

```
var _infoPanel =
    {
      "border":"2px solid black",
      "position":"fixed",
      "background":"white",
      "border-radius": "10px 10px 10px 10px"
    }

var _infoImage =
    {
      "border":"1px solid grey",
```

```
            "border-radius": "10px 10px 10px 10px"
        }

var _infoBoxSeparator =
        {
            "border-bottom":"1px solid grey",
            "padding":"5px",
            "background":"33CCCC",
            "border-radius": "10px 10px 10px 10px"
        }

var _infoTitle =
        {
            "font": "bold 24px Times, Courier, monospace",
            "padding":"5px"
        }

var _infoDescription =
        {
            "font": "normal 14px Times, Courier, monospace",
            "padding":"5px"
        }

var _links =
        {
            "font": "bold 18px Times, Courier, monospace",
            "padding":"5px"
        }
```

Each variable is a style object. In the UI several elements can have the same style assigned and changes to that style apply globally. Now how to apply the CSS?

Because each style must be applied individually a function will iterate each property in the style object and apply it to the given element.

```
function applyCSS(element, style){
  for (var key in style){
    element.setStyleAttribute(key, style[key]);
  }
}
```

Tagging the elements is a bit of work but once finished it has all the benefits of CSS. To start applying style to the images and title links on the products page, insert the following code before the closing } of the products loop.

```
applyCSS(image, _infoImage);
applyCSS(title, _links);
```

Both image and the title have two styles and there are six products so a savings of 20 or so lines of code is a good thing. In the onInfo function after the line infoPanel.add(description); apply more style:

```
applyCSS(infoPanel, _infoPanel);
applyCSS(image, _infoImage);
applyCSS(horzPanel, _infoBoxSeparator);
```

```
applyCSS(title, _infoTitle);
applyCSS(description, _infoDescription);
```

Making things pretty is great but CSS can also move things on the page. The info panel should appear over the other products and by the product that is moused over. This could be done by setting a the position to fixed and then hardcoding a value someplace in the middle of the application. The problem comes when the product list is long requiring scrolling down the page. If you set the info panel to stick at say 100px from the top and left the user would need to scroll back up to see it and that would defeat the effect.

Just like when the product images were loaded and placed in a certain column, the same variables and loop will be used to determine the pixel location for the info panel.

Back in the onInfo function add variables r and c before the products loop. Set r to 50 so the info panel is not shoved up against the top of the page.

```
var r = 50;
var c = 0;
```

Incrementing the location variables is done at the end of the products loop but outside the if statement, between the closing brackets; for{...if {...}right here}

```
c++
if (c == 3){
    c = 0;
    r = r+350;
}
```

The reason 350 is added to r is this works out to be the height of the images plus padding thus moving the info box down the page each time a new row is needed. Moving the image down the page is a good start but it should also move across the page as well. c told us which column to put images in and it can also help determine the pixels from the left to move the info box. The value of c can be 0, 1, or 2. Tou may think that an "if then" loop is in order but JavaScript has a better option, the switch.

A switch is used when you have more than two possible choices and you know the values.

```
switch (c)
    {
    case 0:
        c=250;
        break;
    case 1:
        c=500;
        break;
    case 2:
        c=250;
        break;
    }
```

This switch says that if c is a 1 c=500

The final part of the code will help wrap this up:

```
var _infoLocation =
    {
      "top":r+"px",
      "left":c+"px",
    }
applyCSS(infoPanel, _infoLocation);
```

A special style object is placed here because the script will be in control of setting it not you. In the style px is appended to the values of r and c to create valid top and left coordinates. Run that through applyCSS and the info panel will move to the right place as see in Figure 5-10.

Figure 5-10. Seen in its final state, CSS has been applied to improve the look and position elements.

Delivering the Application

Your application is finished just in time to save the company from sliding into obscurity. With the new interactive interface customers are throwing buckets of money into purchasing your products and even Frank's boss is looking to advance you to a VP title.

Well it's all a nice thought but welcome back to reality. The application you have built certainly looks great and it allows different styling from the CSS file meaning a fresh look is little work on your part. On the backend the database is easy for anyone to use allowing products to be added or removed and product page templates generated automatically. It is a full system that is portable and can easily be setup for different product databases.

You have also learned some important techniques like; loading data from or writing it to a spreadsheet and applying CSS to UiApp elements. This knowledge will be useful as you progress into more advanced applications.

Up next, you will build an application that goes out into the world to find information and brings it back for a mashup that will keep you in the know.

CHAPTER 6

Automate Your Forms and Templates

If your business is like most, it has forms lying everywhere to get this process or that request done. Most of the time these forms are the same thing over and over with a few things changed out. Letters to say thank you for a purchase, patient intake, and filing with the court are all examples of situations when we might encounter a form. Now I certainly would like to see everything in tidy data structures, but in reality we need forms to ground us in that paper, human readable format; that is not going anywhere soon.

Google Apps gives us a great platform for collaboration, storage, and creation of documentation. However, there really is not a way to create forms that generate a nice print style page layout that is easy to distribute.

The Forms feature in Google Spreadsheets is a great way to collect information; it uses a web page style form that anyone who has ever used a computer can understand. This feature fills in a spreadsheet, making it is good tool for collection and analysis, but not for the output of a document, like your taxes. Another option is to build a template in Google Documents, leaving blank lines for where you would like certain things filled in. But what about extra instructions and the worry of a certain field getting missed? You could fire up Word and spend the next week trying to get the form field insert function to work and the next year explaining to users how to use it, but you know they will make a copy on their hard drive that will come back to haunt you from seven revisions ago.

This chapter will go down a new road using Google Documents and Script to form a system that takes a template and automatically generates a web form for your users to fill out.

What You Will Learn

How to:

- Edit Google Docs from a script

- Create new documents using the DocsList service
- Work with template keys
- Generate a web form from text in a document

Supplies

You will need:

- A Template document (created during the chapter)
- Spreadsheet or Site to hold the script

Application Overview

In this chapter, we are going to use the power of Google Script to add functionality to Google Docs by building an application that will allow you to choose a template in your Document Collections and have the script automatically create a web form from key values you specify in the document. Not only will your web form be complete with instructions, the script is smart enough to remove the instructions from the final copy. Filling out the form and submitting it will create a copy of the template, replace the template key fields with the answers on the form, and save the new copy in your Google Docs. You can extend this company-wide or even to the public, allowing for easy creation of common documents. The script is set up to generate a form for any template you provide it, so once set up, adding or changing forms is all done in Google Documents and no further coding is required.

Setting Up the Template

Templates come in every shape and size, and the information that needs to be replaced usually has some sort of key that tells you to replace it with your information. For example, if you migrated over to Google Apps, there are documents produced by Google to help you tell your users what to expect, or to answer frequently asked questions. In these documents you will see red text in brackets that says things like, "<your company name>". This is called a key, and it's how our script will figure out what a key is.

You can create keys any way you like, but for this book {%Your Key%} will be used. Therefore, if you would like to personalize the salutation, use Dear {%Recipient%}, in the form. There will also be a special instruction key that is used to display information to the user about what they see on the screen. Instructions look like this: {%Instruction:This is an automated template example.%}. When the script sees that a key starts with Instruction, it will know not to create a text box for user input and to remove that paragraph from the final document.

A template for this chapter with formatting can be found here (*https://docs.google.com/ document/d/18WZTBHAI5P-eAesevdwdWihTeUOYGSkDXsMgkSm5h9k/edit*); use File and make a copy.

 If you can't access the document linked above, here is an example that will work fine in your own document:

If you have ever been a kid, you likely filled out a Mad Lib. Let's give that a try here in this template.

{%Instruction: Please fill in the words below for your Mad Lib example. %}

{%Exclamation%}! he said {%Adverb%} as he jumped into his convertible {%Noun%} and {%Verb%} off with his {%Adjective%} wife.

{%Instruction:An exclamation is the act of exclaiming; outcry; loud complaint, or protest. Examples include Ouch and Dang.%}

{%Instruction:A noun is the name of a person, place, or thing. Examples include umbrella, sidewalk, telephone, and policeman.%}

{%Instruction:An adjective describes someone or something. Examples include creative, red, ugly, and short.%}

{%Instruction:A verb is an action word. Examples include run, jump, swim, and fly.%}

{%Instruction:An adverb tells how something is done. It modifies a verb, and usually ends in "ly." Examples include greedily, rapidly, modestly, and carefully.%}

Make sure each instruction has its own paragraph because the script will remove them.

You can use any formating you like and it will be carried over when the keys are replaced. This means you can have keys as document headers, in tables, and certainly color, bold, italic, etc. Adding formatting really does give a polished look to the final document.

After creating your template, put it in a collection just for templates. This way, when we display a drop down list for the user to choose from, he will only get templates and not every other file in your Docs list.

Building the Script

Now that the form is ready to be filled out, it is time to build the script. Open a new spreadsheet, save it, and name it. Create a new script named Dynamic Templates, or some other fitting name of your choosing.

UI Setup

This will be a basic UI with very few elements that you need to write in the code, however, the UI can fill itself with a hundred questions if that is what is in the template. The code does the work and makes you look like a coding genius.

When the UI loads, doGet runs and builds a grid to hold the elements. See Figure 6-1.

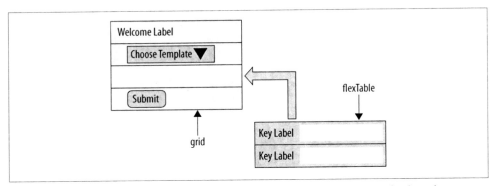

Figure 6-1. Cell (3,0) is automatically filled with the template key questions on list box change.

As the script administrator, you will need to set up a specific collection in Google Documents and share it with your domain. Note the collection ID in the URL in the address bar; you will need this to get the files from that folder. A specific collection gives you a place to create templates and update them as needed. The script will list all Google Documents in that collection, so it is best to think about it as being public. You can certainly restrict access to the documents there so they can't be edited, but your script will have unrestricted access to the files.

In the default *code* file, you will need a global variable to hold the ID of your template collection.

 Global variables are created outside of any function and can be accessed from anywhere in your script. You can update them as the script runs, but remember that when the UI is reloaded, they are set back to the original value.

Now create the UiApp and publish it. Take special care in publishing a script that has access to your Documents; set the level of sharing appropriately and load a page with the published URL.

```
var templateFolderId = 'Your_Collection_ID';

function doGet(e){
  var app = UiApp.createApplication().setTitle('Template Creator');
```

```
    //create UI here

    return app;
  }
```

The **grid** will hold all of the elements in the UI, set its padding to give some room around the edges, and add it to the UI.

Optional, but a good idea, is to add a label to tell the user what this application is all about:

```
var grid = app.createGrid(6, 2).setId('grid').setCellPadding(5);
app.add(grid);

grid.setWidget(0,0, app.createLabel("This App will allow you to create a form from"+
                            " a template in Google Docs."));
```

The next item to load is the list box that will show the files in the templates folder. Be sure to set its name and ID and add a change handler so that the script reacts to the user changing a value. The **showForm** function, to be created soon, will run on change. Because the script will need to place information in other parts of the **grid**, you will want to add it as the callback element.

```
// File Chooser
  var fileChooser = app.createListBox().setName('fileChooser').setId('fileChooser')
                    .addChangeHandler(app.createServerChangeHandler('showForm')
                    .addCallbackElement(grid));
  grid.setWidget(2, 0, fileChooser);
```

The first item added to a list box is what the user will see when they load the UI. So they know to take action, we add the first value as "Choose Template". The DocsList service will give you access to the files in your Google Documents.

 Don't mix up DocsList with DocumentApp. Both give access to Google Documents, but the list service is for working with the files while the document service is for editing the content of documents.

Use the **getFolderById** method to get the folder and **getFiles** to return an array of the files in the folder. Iterate the array getting the name of each file and adding that to the list box.

```
//set the file Names in the listBox by calling on the DocsList service
  fileChooser.addItem('Choose Template');
  var files = DocsList.getFolderById(templateFolderId).getFiles();
  for (var i = 0; i < files.length; i++) {
    fileChooser.addItem(files[i].getName());
  }
```

After the template values have been returned to the UI, a button will be used to create a new document and insert the form values from the UI. The button will execute the function **createDoc** and, like the list box, it calls back to grid.

Set the visibility to false so the user won't see it until the UI has a form ready to fill out:

```
// Submit the form button
   var button = app.createButton('Submit').setId('button')
                    .addClickHandler(app.createServerClickHandler('createDoc')
                              .addCallbackElement(grid))
                    .setVisible(false);

   grid.setWidget(4, 0, button);
```

Click Run to grant access for Google Documents and go to the published page. Figure 6-2 shows the list box with a template to choose.

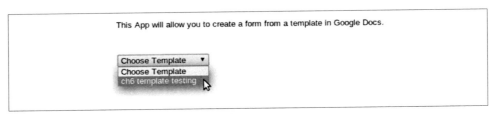

Figure 6-2. Documents listed from your Google account

Adding Helpers

When you write your templates, you want the template key to be useful to the user when determining what a field is in order to fill it out. However, we also need that key value to represent a certain text box name. As discussed in Chapter 5 on JavaScript save values, you know that Your Email Address will look good in the form but will cause an error as the name of a text box. Conversely, yourEmailAddress is not, depending on the user, going to win you points with coworkers as they try to decrypt your form.

Again we will call on the ever useful GS Objects Class (*https://sites.google.com/site/ scriptsexamples/custom-methods/gs-objects/source*) to do some cameling for the variable text. Create a new file named **GS Objects** and copy in the source. You can close that file to get it out of the way; there is nothing to do there.

At the time of this writing, Google Script was not open to get text from a Google Document, only text and CSV. Unfortunately, you can't edit those document types in Google Docs. We need to get the text from the template and parse it for keys so we know what to put in the form; not having access is a game stopper. But for places Google Script can't yet go, we have the urlFetchApp service.

If you know much about the Google APIs, you may have run across one called Google Documents List API (*http://code.google.com/apis/documents/*), which has access to every aspect of Documents and speaks in JSON, a language the urlFetchApp understands. It can't directly edit like the Google Script DocumentApp, but it can download in several formats including text, which will work well for our parsing of key values.

Create a new file named Documents API.

I don't want to sugar coat connecting to authenticated services using urlFetchApp and OAuth; it can be a tricky and a frustrating experience, but the two methods we are going to build next work perfectly using the GData API 3.0, saving you hours of trouble.

The first method will take care of the authentication and uses the OAuth service, so you won't need to expose your password over the Web. Copy the code below into your script as is, but note that this is specific to Documents.

```
/*
 * Private for OAuth
 * @ returns OAuth headers
 */
DOCS_LIST_API.googleOAuth = function() {
  var oAuthConfig = UrlFetchApp.addOAuthService('google');
  oAuthConfig.setRequestTokenUrl("https://www.google.com/accounts/"+
          "OAuthGetRequestToken?scope=https://docs.google.com/feeds/");
  oAuthConfig.setAuthorizationUrl("https://www.google.com/accounts/
OAuthAuthorizeToken");
  oAuthConfig.setAccessTokenUrl("https://www.google.com/accounts/
OAuthGetAccessToken");
  oAuthConfig.setConsumerKey('anonymous');
  oAuthConfig.setConsumerSecret('anonymous');
  return {oAuthServiceName:'google', oAuthUseToken:"always"};
}
```

 To most Google services, authenticating looks like the code above. The main difference is the scope and service name. Setting the consumer key and secret to anonymous will bring up the special grant access screens in Google Script.

The next method will return the file as a blob. This is very useful if you want to email a file as a different format not supported as a conversion type in Google Script, which is everything but .pdf:

```
var DOCS_LIST_API = {};

/*
 * @ args      docID  String   the id for a Google Document
 * @ args      format String   can be, "txt", "odt", "pdf", "html", "rtf", "doc", "png",
 "zip"
 * @ returns   blob
 *
 */
DOCS_LIST_API.GdocToFormat = function(docID, format){
  var fetchArgs = DOCS_LIST_API.googleOAuth();
  fetchArgs.headers = { "GData-Version": "3.0" };
  fetchArgs.method = 'get';
  var url = 'https://docs.google.com/feeds/download/documents/export/Export?id='+
                  docID+'&exportFormat='+format+'&format='+format;
  return UrlFetchApp.fetch(url, fetchArgs);
}
```

You only need to authenticate once for the script and that will remain in your account settings. To get the authentication out of the way now we will use a quick function to run DOCS_LIST_API.GdocToFormat:

```
// Run it twice
function doOAuth(){
  try{
    DOCS_LIST_API.GdocToFormat();
  }catch(e){
  }
}
```

Save the script, then choose doOAuth from the Run menu, and run it. You will see the typical Google Script Grant access box (See Figure 6-3) that you see when you add services.

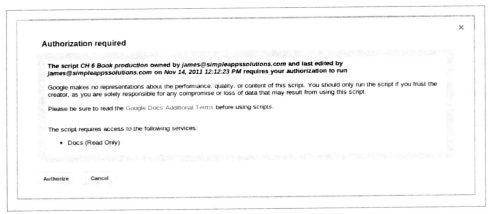

Figure 6-3. This screen is for the file created in Google Script

Now run the function a second time. You will see a new smaller window asking you to authorize (See Figure 6-4).

Figure 6-4. This window is for the Documents List API

After clicking Authorize, you will be asked to grant access to your Google Docs along with a big scary yellow warning, shown in Figure 6-5. You should always read what

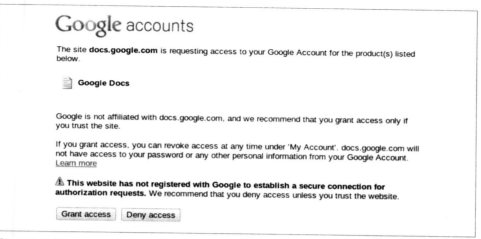

Google accounts

The site **docs.google.com** is requesting access to your Google Account for the product(s) listed below.

📄 **Google Docs**

Google is not affiliated with docs.google.com, and we recommend that you grant access only if you trust the site.

If you grant access, you can revoke access at any time under 'My Account'. docs.google.com will not have access to your password or any other personal information from your Google Account. Learn more

⚠ **This website has not registered with Google to establish a secure connection for authorization requests.** We recommend that you deny access unless you trust the website.

Grant access   Deny access

Figure 6-5. Here you grant access to your script

these warnings say, but in this case, it is your script accessing your account. Keep in mind what it means when making a UI application public.

After clicking "Grant Access," your script is now authorized to use the Google Documents List API.

Getting the Keys

Back over in the Code file, we are going to put those new methods to work by writing a function that gets the text from a Google Doc using the DocsList API.

 This script only allows for uniquely named files in your templates folder. This should not be much of a problem, but is something to keep in mind.

Assuming we know the name of the file, we will get the files in the folder like we did for the list box and then iterate through them to find a matching name. Once we know what file the user wants, we can get its ID using `.getId()`. That gets passed into the `DOCS_LIST_API.GdocToFormat` you created in "Adding Helpers" on page 76 as the first argument. We specify `txt` so that the returning blob will be plain text and return the text content as a string:

```
/*
 *  @returns body text from doc
 */
function getTemplateText(fileName){
  var files = DocsList.getFolderById(templateFolderId).getFiles();
    for (var i = 0; i < files.length; i++) {
      if (fileName == files[i].getName()){
        var text = DOCS_LIST_API.GdocToFormat(files[i].getId(), 'txt');
```

```
        return text.getContentText();
      }
    }
  }
```

Great! Now we have a string containing all the text in the template. All we need now is to parse out the keys.

The next function to add in the Code file will return a set of keys in an array that looks like this: [{text:'Key One', id:'keyOne'},{...}].

This is done by matching the key's unique identifiers {%Key%} and placing them into an array. At the same time, the key is cameled so that it can be used as a JavaScript name or ID. We only want one of each value in case the template does something like ask for a person's name and uses the same key over and over. You don't want the form to render a text box for repeated keys; once will do just fine.

```
// function returns an array of unique form keys
function createKeys(templateFile){
  var templateTxt = getTemplateText(templateFile);
  var templateVars = templateTxt.match(/\{\%[^\%]+\%\}/g);
  var templateKeys = [];
  var oneEach = "";
  for (var i in templateVars) {
    var keyObject = {};
    keyObject.text = templateVars[i].replace(/\{\%|\%\}/g, '');
    keyObject.id = camelString(templateVars[i]);
    if (oneEach.match(keyObject.text) == null){
      templateKeys.push(keyObject);
    }
    oneEach += " " + keyObject.text;
  }
  return templateKeys;
}
```

Generating the Form

In the last sections, you created the functions to get the data from the different Google services. Now you can put those to good use.

When you select a template from the list box, it will execute the showForm function. Add the showForm function to the Code file and because it is executed by a handler, don't forget to put an e in the arguments so you can gain access to the selection in the list box.

This function will return a flex table containing the keys from the template, so get the active application and create a flex table.

Next get the keys from the chosen template using e.parameter.fileChooser to get the template name; pass that through createKeys. The getTemplateText function runs shortly after like a cascade of functions. The end result is an array containing the keys as text and their matching JavaScript safe counterparts.

```
function showForm(e){
    var app = UiApp.getActiveApplication();
    var flexTable = app.createFlexTable();
    var keys = createKeys(e.parameter.fileChooser);
```

Now that the keys are ready to go, you can build the UI form. What looks like it might take hours to perform actually boils down to about 14 lines of code, but can make an endless number of fields to fill out.

Start iterating through the keys array and building a label for the text of the key and a text box right next to it. To shorten up the typing, turn the current keys[i].text into a new string text.

Before creating labels and text boxes, you need to find out if the template key is an instruction. When the template is created, you have the option of adding Instruc tion: to the beginning of a key. Here in the script we use a regular expression to see if the key begins with Instruction: in both upper and lower case. If the test is true, we will only make a label because instructions don't get answers.

> If your templates require other treatment such as creating multiple choice questions or formatting to highlight a section, you would simply add more tests and adjust the template. Try out a Section:Title and add a background for the label using .setStyleAttribute('background', '#A0A0A0').
>
> You can also make questions go across the page using the horizontal counter techniques in Chapter 4.

You likely don't want it to say "Instruction" at the beginning, so everything before and including the colon is stripped off using the substring method.

If no special test fits the key then it must be a regular question, which gets the label/ text box recipe. Using a horizontal panel and adding the two elements is quick and easy; if you set the width of the label, everything gets nicely aligned on the page.

When the text box is created make sure to set the key's ID as the name of that box. Later this value will be read from e.parameter for its value.

```
for (var i in keys) {
  var text = (keys[i].text);

  if(/^instruction/i.test(text)){
    flexTable.setWidget(parseInt(i),0,app
                        .createLabel(text.substring(text.indexOf(':')+1)));
  }else{
    var questionPanel = app.createHorizontalPanel();
    flexTable.setWidget(parseInt(i),0,questionPanel);
    questionPanel.add(app.createLabel(text).setWidth('100px'));
    questionPanel.add(app.createTextBox().setName(keys[i].id));
  }
}
```

That is all there is to displaying the template keys and building the UI, but there are a few more things to add before handing back the flex table. We will give the user an opportunity to name their copy of the template and open it from a link. Because the new document is created under your account, the user will not be able to access it. Therefore, we need to ask the user for their Google email address. A better technique for Google Apps domains will be discussed later in "Delivery Options" on page 85.

To get additional information that was not on the form, use the length of the key to find the last row in the flex table and add 1. Continue to add elements for the information required:

```
flexTable.setWidget(keys.length+1,0,app.createLabel('_____'));
flexTable.setWidget(keys.length+2,0, app.createHorizontalPanel()
                              .add(app.createLabel('Output file name:
').setWidth('100px'))
                                 .add(app.createTextBox()
                                     .setName('outputFile').setWidth('200px')
                                 .setValue('Copy of '+ e.parameter.fileChooser)));
flexTable.setWidget(keys.length+3,0, app.createHorizontalPanel()
                              .add(app.createLabel('Google Email:
').setWidth('100px'))
                                 .add(app.createTextBox()
                                     .setName('email').setWidth('200px')));
```

When the UI loaded, the Submit button was hidden. You can now show it to the user by changing its visibility. The flex table is now full of content and can be placed back in the grid by getting the grid by ID and using the setWidget method:

```
app.getElementById('button').setVisible(true);
app.getElementById('grid').setWidget(3,0, flexTable);

return app;
}
```

Once the app returns, the UI will update with your template information, as shown in Figure 6-6. Make sure you have authorized everything by clicking Run, and then reload the published page. Like magic, your Google Docs Template has magically transformed into a web form.

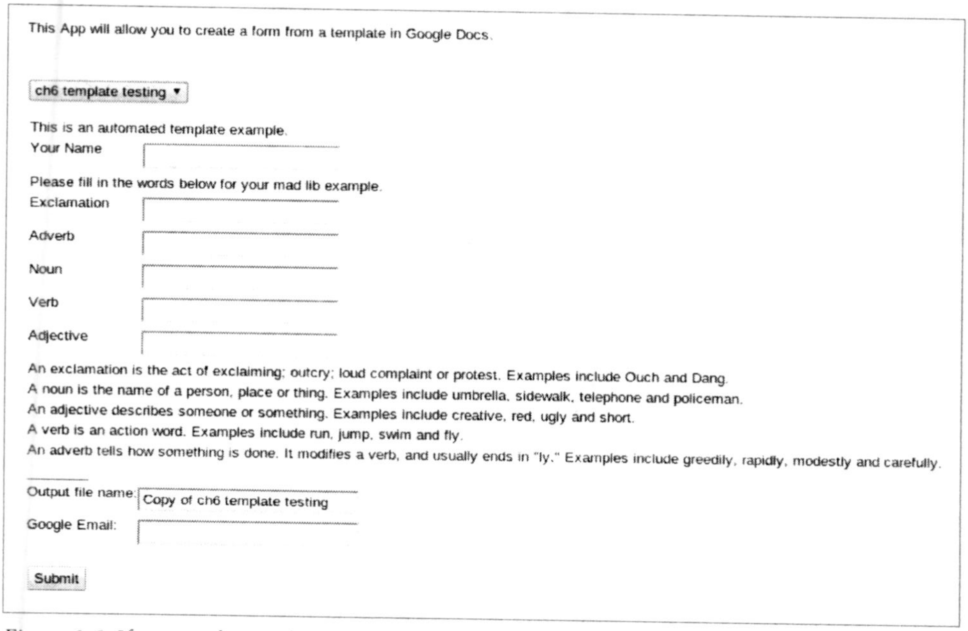

This App will allow you to create a form from a template in Google Docs.

[ch6 template testing ▼]

This is an automated template example.
Your Name [_____]

Please fill in the words below for your mad lib example.
Exclamation [_____]

Adverb [_____]

Noun [_____]

Verb [_____]

Adjective [_____]

An exclamation is the act of exclaiming; outcry; loud complaint or protest. Examples include Ouch and Dang.
A noun is the name of a person, place or thing. Examples include umbrella, sidewalk, telephone and policeman.
An adjective describes someone or something. Examples include creative, red, ugly and short.
A verb is an action word. Examples include run, jump, swim and fly.
An adverb tells how something is done. It modifies a verb, and usually ends in "ly." Examples include greedily, rapidly, modestly and carefully.

Output file name: [Copy of ch6 template testing]
Google Email: [_____]

[Submit]

Figure 6-6. If you need more formatting simply add test conditions.

Copy the Template and Add Responses

The application is running great and rendering templates as web forms. Changing the file in the list box will update the page with a new template. It may seem like we are only halfway done, but in reality it will only take one more function to wrap everything up.

The createDoc function is executed when the Submit button is pressed and is the last function in the application. Create the createDoc in the Code file and get the active application.

Like you did when building the UI, get the keys again from the template. Now get the files in the templates folder:

```
function createDoc(e){

    var app = UiApp.getActiveApplication();
    var keys = createKeys(e.parameter.fileChooser);
    var files = DocsList.getFolderById(templateFolderId).getFiles();
```

We don't know the ID of the file, so iterate the files array for a matching name. Once the match is found, make a copy using the DocumentsList service and name it what the user specified on the form. This value should be in e.parameter.outputFile. Lastly, get the copy's ID, which is used in the next line to open the document from the Doc-umentApp for editing.

You need to get the active selection, which at this time is the whole document. Now iterate over the keys. When a line of text starting with "Instruction" matches the regular expression in the if statement, that line is removed from the text string. The standard keys get replaced by the text value from the form using `e.parameter[keys[i].id]` where the ID for the key was used to name the text box.

To give the user access to the document, add them as an editor:

```
for (var i in files) {
    if (e.parameter.fileChooser == files[i].getName()){
        var copyId = files[i].makeCopy(e.parameter.outputFile).getId();
        var doc = DocumentApp.openById(copyId)
        var copy = doc.getActiveSection();
        for (var i in keys) {
          var text = keys[i].text;
          if(/^instruction/i.test(text)){
            if (copy.findText(keys[i].text) != null)
              copy.findText(keys[i].text).getElement().removeFromParent();
          }else{
            copy.replaceText('{%'+keys[i].text+'%}', e.parameter[keys[i].id]);
          }
        }
        doc.saveAndClose();
        doc.addEditor(e.parameter.email);
    }
}
```

That finishes creating the Google Doc and replacing the values; those `findText` and `replaceText` really make short work of it.

Now the UI needs a few updates. Create an anchor so the user can open their new document; the URL is in the doc and you get it with the `getUrl` method. The anchor is placed in the grid at cell (3,0), which is where the form is currently, so the effect is that the form disappears.

Now that the form is gone, we don't want the Submit button to be accessible so it is rehidden. Lastly, reset the list box for the next choice:

```
app.getElementById('grid').setWidget(3,0, app.createAnchor('Open your Document',
doc.getUrl())
                                    .setStyleAttribute('font-size', '18px'));
app.getElementById('button').setVisible(false);
app.getElementById('fileChooser').setItemSelected(0, true);

return app;
}
```

Click Run to authorize and reload the published page.

Select a template and fill out the form. Use your own email address and click Submit. The Open Document link will replace the form, allowing you to open the document. If you have been using the provided template, you should get a chuckle from the Mad Lib. Figure 6-7 shows that the keys have been replaced and the instructions removed.

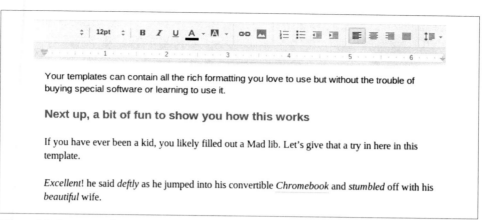

Your templates can contain all the rich formatting you love to use but without the trouble of buying special software or learning to use it.

Next up, a bit of fun to show you how this works

If you have ever been a kid, you likely filled out a Mad lib. Let's give that a try in here in this template.

Excellent! he said *deftly* as he jumped into his convertible <u>Chromebook</u> and *stumbled* off with his *beautiful* wife.

Figure 6-7. Document formatting stays intact after replacing the keys

Delivery Options

The application is completed and will work perfectly in most situations. However, there are a few things that could be improved with the delivery. First, we ask for the user's email. If our templates will only be used in our own domain, this step can be skipped completely by using the Session to tell us which user is on the page.

Getting the user's email address will only work with a domain, or Google Apps account.

On the same domain remove the Google email text box and change the line:

```
doc.addEditor(e.parameter.email);
```

to use the Session user:

```
doc.addEditor(Session.getActiveUser().getEmail());
```

Now this part of the process will be seamless for the user.

If you are providing a public service, your users may not have a Google account, making sharing of the document in the Editor impossible. The best solution for this scenario is to send the finished template as an email. Where you would normally add the Editor, instead create and send an email:

```
copyDoc.saveAndClose();
//create a pdf blob
var pdf = DocsList.getFileById(copyId).getAs("application/pdf");
//send the email
MailApp.sendEmail(e.parameter.email, 'Auto Forms', 'See Attached', {attachments:
pdf});
    DocsList.getFileById(copyId).setTrashed(true);
```

This method will allow you to distribute custom forms to anyone. Dress up the email body with some HTML and you have a great public-facing application capable of serving out all sorts of forms. This makes me wonder why more government agencies don't get on Google Apps just for this feature alone. We can all hope, but in the meantime, enjoy impressing your coworkers with the magic of auto forms.

CHAPTER 7

Collecting Data

It was a fine mess they had gotten themselves into. Scattered across the country, databases in various states of update and version, but not one location knew what the other was doing or if they could count on the "main hub" to be accurate with data that was less than a year out of date. That's when they called you.

Certainly you are the expert they placed all their hope on who could bring the worn and tired infrastructure back from the grave. As you gaze into the endless abyss filled with the rot and decay from a thousand rickshaw contractors all with dreams of a quick buck for adding another band aid to the hemorrhaging artery, you realize that those days of the local copy are over and you will be the one to usher in a new era.

The Installed App Has Died

You can only wish that your coworkers saw you as a hero saving them from all the problems they are likely to inflict on themselves, but the truth is they will likely never know what goes into making a database work or the hardship of keeping it running. Fortunately, times are changing and the days of building a frontend, installing it, maintaining it, and trying to keep everyone connected are rapidly coming to an end. The internal network has been replaced by the Internet and cellular networks extend connections far beyond the reach of copper.

Today's databases are hosted in massive data centers that never fail to serve requests and cost almost nothing for the storage. Frontend "installed" applications have been replaced by a browser and connections are made globally. The data is always in sync because it is all in the same place, or appears to be, as the great hosts handle cross data center transfers in millisecond time.

Why is this good for your database building career? Simple, when you get ready to build your next database, you won't be thinking about servers and backups—those are covered by the host—rather your thoughts should fall on how well your application will perform on the next generation of smartphones and language support. Having a roll-out plan does not include installing software or worrying over the type of equipment it runs on, because if your client has a browser, they run your software.

This chapter is about building a simple web-based database application. The entire application will be hosted within the Google Documents service using Fusion Tables and Google Script. Because the user interface is hosted on the Web, changes you make are reflected in real time to everyone.

What You Will Learn

How to:

- Work with multiple panel views
- Use components
- Retrieve a specific record
- Work with Fusion Tables
- Create a basic database layout
- Use contextual buttons
- Generate OAuth and client authentication
- Use urlFetchApp
- Automatically generate form fields
- Use Script Properties

Supplies

You will need:

- Google Fusion Table
- Google Script

Application Overview

This application will use the Google Script standalone UI style and be sized to work well on smaller screens, like on a phone or tablet, but not too small to look out of place when running as a gadget in a Google Site. When the application is loaded in the browser, the user will be presented with a welcome panel (See Figure 7-1) and options to search the records or create a new record.

Searching will connect to a Fusion Table that holds the records and returns the results as a table to the content area where the welcome image had been. There are mouse over effects for the result rows and clicking a result will open that record for viewing (text fields disabled) and an edit button will be added to the menu. Clicking Edit will unlock

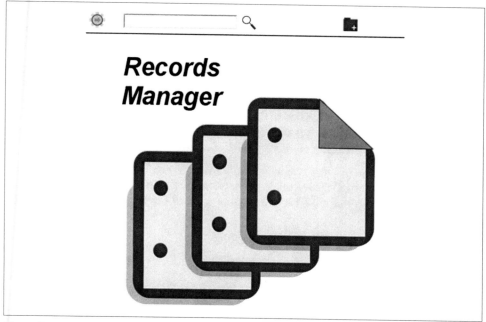

Figure 7-1. Users expect to see something when an application loads to let them know it's ready.

the fields, and the Edit button will be replaced Save and Cancel buttons. Cancel resets the fields and goes back to View mode. Save writes changes to the Fusion Table. New records load a blank form and an Insert Record button.

From the description you can guess that this is a typical database application with the only real difference being the hosted web service and data storage. The model we use will be flexible in that no additional coding is needed to add or remove database fields; they are automatically generated from the Fusion Table. The script will also be portable, meaning that given a few key search fields the script can be pointed at any Fusion Table and work out of the box.

Setting Up

Big scripts, or applications, can consume thousands of lines of code, so having a plan is necessary to keep you organized. One of the first things you should create is a file to hold all of the items that will be used script-wide.

 In a Google Script, any variables outside of a function will be global and accessible anywhere in the script. Best practice says that because Java-Script is a top down language, any global variables should go at the beginning of the script ensuring they will be available when called.

You can name your files whatever you like, but always keep in mind that you may need to come back to your application years from now and leaving plenty of information about where things are will save you hours walking back through the code in the future.

Open up a new Google Script; it does not matter where because this will be a standalone application. Save the script as **Record Manager** and rename the **Code** file to **Settings**. If you later decide that was not the name you wanted, it can be changed from the File menu without causing any problems in the script. Go ahead and delete the sample code; you won't be using that. The Settings file is a good place to keep things like button icons and any images you may want. We will be coming back here to add those soon.

Next create a file called **CSS** where you will hold the style attributes for the whole script. You could also put your CSS objects into the Settings file, but having a dedicated file for CSS is handy and what most developers are used to having. Copy in the `applyCSS` function:

```
function applyCSS_(element, style){
  for (var key in style){
    element.setStyleAttribute(key, style[key]);
  }
}
```

You might be wondering what the underscore before the arguments means. In Google Script, to hide a function from the Run menu in the Editor, use an underscore. This can go a long way in cleaning up your Run menu options but is not otherwise needed.

Because there is nothing to apply CSS to yet, let's move on to the next file: doGet. Every UiApp needs an entrypoint and the **doGet** function is your starting point in Google Script UIs. Create a new file and name it **doGet**, then add the create and return app statements:

```
function doGet(e) {
  var app = UiApp.createApplication().setTitle('Record Manager');

  return app;
}
```

Publish the script with the settings of your choice and load a new tab with the published URL. You are now ready to start building the actual application, but first a few words on design.

Building the Foundation

Honestly, I don't always know where a script is going until writing a few hundred lines of code, but that can lead down some dark alleys and waste time if you don't have a clear picture of where you need to go. A good way to stay on track is to sketch what you think the UI should look like and do. Google Drawings is a quick way to start working on the visual aspects, but you may also find the GUI Builder works very well and has the actual elements you will be working with. You could use the GUI builder to make the opening page view, but after that the elements are going to be added dynamically so the GUI Builder will be of little help. The code in this chapter won't use the GUI Builder so you can see what everything is doing but feel free to start there if it works for you.

Main Panel

Figure 7-2 shows the skeletal layout of the application. At the very bottom of the stack there will be a vertical panel to hold everything and give you a reference point to call on if you need access to certain elements.

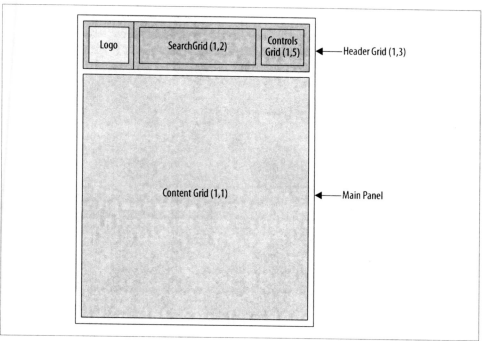

Figure 7-2. Drawing the application saves time and helps show you what will and won't fit.

Add the vertical to **app** thus creating your application canvas:

```
var mainPanel = app.createVerticalPanel();
app.add(mainPanel);
```

Headers Grid

The top most element in the application is a header and contains three areas: the logo, the search function, and buttons to control the application. These options will always be available to the user but the context of the buttons will change depending on the current view. While there are only three areas, nesting widgets will give the application the flexibility it needs.

Add a one-row, three-column grid to the main panel:

```
var headerGrid = app.createGrid(1,3).setId('headerGrid').setWidth('500px');
mainPanel.add(headerGrid);
```

Setting the width here in the headerGrid means that this grid will set the width for the entire application and ensure the header goes all the way across. Don't forget to ID the grid, you might need to call on it later.

To add some separation from the rest of the elements, CSS will be used to put a border on the bottom of the table. This gives the effect of a horizontal line:

```
applyCSS_(headerGrid, _headerGrid);
```

Go back to the CSS file and add an entry for the CSS object _headerGrid. The example will stick to a simple look like what is seen in other Google services, but if you would like more color, go ahead and add a background entry in the CSS:

```
var _headerGrid =
    {
    "border-bottom":"2px solid #404040"
    }
```

Brand It

Branding is important as it gives the application some grounding. When your users come to the application, they notice the logo and it helps them feel comfortable that they are in the right place. You can use any image you want and if you would like to use the images used to write this chapter, they are available at the links in the code examples.

Go to the Settings file and add a link to your logo:

```
var logoImgage = 'https://sites.google.com/site/scriptsexamples/scriptGear.png';
```

The reason you want to put the link here and not in the doGet code is to make it easier to reprovision the application. You only need to look in one place to change the icons and images. That organization is starting to pay off.

In the doGet file, create a new image widget and set its size. This will keep things under control if the logo image is changed out:

```
var logo = app.createImage(logoImgage).setSize('30px', '30px');
```

Note how the variable logoImage is accessed here even though it is not in the doGet function. The logo belongs in the upper-left corner of the header, which happens to be grid cell (0,0).

```
headerGrid.setWidget(0,0,logo);
```

Now that you have a few elements to look at, take a break and reload the published URL.

Loading the Search Component

The next part to add to the application is the record search function. Like any search box there will be a text box to type in the search words and a button to click that executes the search. Additionally, if the user hits the "Enter" key, the search should also be performed. These widgets and their handlers are a self-contained chunk of code that can be thought of as a component.

When building a complex application, finding ways to make components will save time and make the code easier to read. Think of it as having an engine ready to go for your car. The car won't go without the engine and the engine can't run without input—gas —from the car's tank. Instead of putting all the parts of the engine in the car permanently, they are added as an engine component that can get swapped out for something with more power.

In Google Script, it makes sense to store components in a file of their own. Create a new file called **Search Component** and replace the default code with a new function:

```
function loadSearchBox(app) {

}
```

Note that the argument **app** is being passed into the function. This is done in order to build widgets from the current app object that has not yet returned to the user.

 When the UiApp loads a page, it can't call on a handler. Therefore you must pass the UiApp instance to any function that will be loading elements on the page. Calling UiApp.getActiveApplication within a function will not work because the original instance has not returned to the browser.

The best widget choice for this Search Component is a grid. This will allow plugging in other widgets into the cells from anywhere in the script if needed. With a component, you don't return the app object but the widget that was created. Again this code could have been completely written in the doGet, so think of it as remotely creating the object. Thinking back to using Java in Eclipse, there was a cool menu function that would move a chunk of code like this to a method.

```
var searchGrid = app.createGrid(1,3).setId('searchGrid');

return searchGrid;
```

Figure 7-3 shows the different parts that will need to go into building the component. There is a text box, and a button or image if you like, that go into building this component.

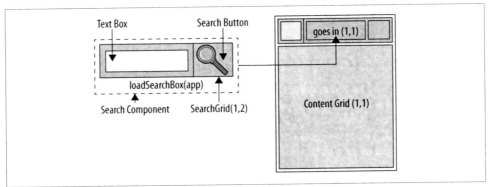

Figure 7-3. Components are sets of smaller parts that always go together and plug into the larger application.

The text box goes in cell (0,0) of the searchGrid and has a handler that fires on each key press. Its function, searchView, will wait for key code 13 (Enter key), and then load another component to the content grid. More on that just ahead.

```
var searchBox = app.createTextBox()
    .setName('searchBox')
    .setId('searchBox')
    .addKeyUpHandler(app.createServerKeyHandler('searchView')
    .addCallbackElement(searchBox));
searchGrid.setWidget(0,0, searchBox);
```

The text box name and ID are both set so that the value entered by the user can be passed through the handler in e.parameter. Pressing a key makes an entry when the button is pressed down, therefore a keyUpHandler will be used to ensure the input is captured. The callback is the text box itself because that is the only thing we need to perform a search.

Most users will hit the Enter key after typing, but if there is not a way to tell the user what that text box does, they may become confused. The magnifying glass is well known and a good choice if you would like to have an image. A button labeled "Search" is also effective and less work to create.

Because we want this application to have a nice visual appeal, images designed by the author will be used for the buttons. You are free to use them in any of your applications. Switch over to the Settings file and add the search icon URL:

```
var searchIcon = 'https://sites.google.com/site/scriptsexamples/searchicon.png';
```

Now add the image to cell (0,1) of the searchGrid and add a clickHandler similar to the keyHandler on the text box. Don't forget to set the size, it would be unfortunate to have a four inch tall magnifying glass.

```
var searchButton = app.createImage(searchIcon)
    .setSize('25px', '25px')
    .setId('searchButton')
    .addClickHandler(app.createServerClickHandler('searchView')
```

```
            .addCallbackElement(searchBox));
    searchGrid.setWidget(0,1, searchButton);
```

In the doGet file, add a line to load the search component into the header grid.

```
    headerGrid.setWidget(0,1, loadSearchBox(app)); //Search component
```

Modular building can yield the benefit of knowing something works and moving on. Go ahead and reload the published page to see where you are. Typing in the box or clicking the button will cause an error because of the missing searchView function, but you should see your component has loaded.

Controls Component

Now that you have built one component, the next one will be a snap. The last cell in the headerGrid is for the buttons that allow a user to create a new record or edit and save existing records. Again, a grid is the best tool so the location of each button can be placed and replaced if necessary.

Create a new file named **Navigation Component** and add the code to create a grid six cells wide to accommodate all the buttons.

```
function loadNavigation(app) {
    var navPanel = app.createGrid(1,6).setId('navPanel');
    var newFileButton = app.createImage(newFileIcon)
        .setSize('25px', '25px')
        .setId('newFileButton')
        .addClickHandler(app.createServerClickHandler('viewRecord'));
    navPanel.setWidget(0,0, newFileButton);
    return navPanel;
}
```

For now there is just one button, but more will be dynamically added later depending on the context of the application. Don't forget to add a link for the icon in Settings:

```
    var newFileIcon = 'https://sites.google.com/site/scriptsexamples/newFileIcon.png';
```

The component is ready to be loaded into the header.

```
    headerGrid.setWidget(0,2,loadNavigation(app)); //Navigation component
```

Content Area

Now that the header is loaded, it is time to start thinking about the content. What the user sees will depend on what they are doing in the application. For example, when loading the page, a welcome image should be the first thing they see. Next they might search and get several records where clicking a specific record shows just that record's details. These different states can be thought of as views. Therefore, a Search view will show search results, a Record view may have many other views such as Edit and View Only. These are all going to be displayed in the single-celled contentGrid.

You might be asking yourself, "Why only one cell?" The answer is the same concept used for the header: build components and swap them out in the same grid location to give the user many views in the same space. Another way to think of it is that when the Search button is clicked, the script builds a search results component and puts it in the content grid. Then when the user wants a certain record, the script builds a record component and puts it in the same cell in the content grid thus writing over the previous component.

 You can't use panels to switch out component views because they only have add methods and no remove method. If you add a component to a panel and then add another component to the same panel, it will not overwrite the first component but rather get stacked after the first component. This is why a grid is used for creating application views by writing to the same cell.

Creating this magic view manager is simple, just add a 1x1 grid to the main panel:

```
var contentGrid = app.createGrid(1,1).setId('contentGrid').setWidth('100%');
mainPanel.add(contentGrid);
```

The ID is important, as you can imagine, we will be calling on this grid often and setting the width to 100% ensures the area will be as wide as the application.

In this application, the user will always need to decide what to do first so instead of having a big blank area, let's give them a splash screen.

Add an image link in Settings:

```
var startImage = 'https://sites.google.com/site/scriptsexamples/RecordsKeeper.png';
```

Now create the image widget and load it in the contentGrid:

```
var splash = app.createImage(startImage).setSize('500px', '500px');
contentGrid.setWidget(0,0, splash);
```

That is the end of the doGet function and the shell of the application. Figure 7-1 displays your work up to this point. In the next section you will start pulling data from a Fusion Table and putting some content views into that shiny new space.

Search View

Now that there some items to click, it's time to start wiring up actions and make the application come to life. The Search button is straightforward: click it and it sends the content of the textBox to your function. The textBox is a different story because you want to know when the user is done entering text and is ready to search by hitting Enter. On each key press, the key handler will execute the function and this means you must look at the key that was pressed to see if it was the Enter key.

Loading the search into the content grid will be much like what was done in the header where a component was used. This way the search can be swapped out with other types of views but without the need to change the page.

Start by creating a new file named **Search View** and a function named `searchView`, the name that was specified in the Search button and textBox handlers from the last section.

```
function searchView(e){
  var app = UiApp.getActiveApplication();
  return app;
}
```

The very first thing that must take place is to handle that key press. Each time a key is pressed the function will run, not such a good idea unless you are trying to simulate Google Instant. The problem is that the user experience may not be great if the connection is slow and results don't display right after a key press. We will not attempt instant results here, but if you are interested the best way to go about it is to fetch the results that start with the first letter entered and keep them in an array. Then start providing results after the third letter is entered from the array.

For our application we need to know if it was the Search button or the textBox that executed; that is determined by `e.parameter.source`.

 The values passed by a handler carry some very important properties. `e.parameter.source` will tell you the ID of the widget that executed the handler so you know who is calling. `e.parameter.keyCode` will tell you the key code for a given key, which is how you find the Enter key (the Enter key code is 13, by the way).

An `if` statement helps to figure out what to do given the event that comes into the function. If the Search button was clicked, we could just go ahead and run the function, but what if there was no value entered in the textBox? Later in this section you can figure out why this will return all the results in your database, which may not be desirable. To keep that from happening, check to see if the textBox has a value of nothing (not "Null", that is different; a textBox with nothing entered has a value of `''`, also known as an empty string).

The next check is for the Enter key when the caller is also the textBox. If the conditions are true, empty textBox, or the Search box was not sending the Enter key, then return the app. On the user side of things, it looks like they are just typing in the box.

```
if (e.parameter.source=='searchBox' && e.parameter.keyCode!=13 ||
e.parameter.searchBox=='') {
    return app;
}
```

After entering this code, try out the UI. Typing in the box, pressing Enter, and clicking the Search button doesn't seem to do anything; that is because the app is being returned with no changes. There is no need to have an else part to the if statement; it is sufficient to just send back the call and wait on the next.

Once an acceptable condition has made it past the if gatekeeper, we can assume a list of matching data needs to be returned from the database. This will take a component to build what is almost a mini app inside your application. Create a vertical panel to hold everything that will be returned and inserted in the content grid. You can set values in a widget already loaded in the UI using getElementById.

 Remember getElementById is a one-way street; you can set values but you can't get them. The only way to get a value is to push it through a handler.

One way to understand this is to compare it to ordering at a restaurant. You figure out what you want on the menu and ask the waiter to get it. The waiter heads to the kitchen, gets a plate, and loads it with the food you asked for, then brings it back to the table for your consumption. We need to build the plate along with something to keep the bread from soaking up all the gravy. When you need to add data to a UI, but you don't know how many items it will be, the right tool is a Flex Table. To give things some breathing room, set the cell padding at "5". Call this variable searchHeader because the user will need to know what the data returned means. This first Flex Table will be the headers for the data that is returned on the search.

```
var searchPanel = app.createVerticalPanel();
app.getElementById('contentGrid').setWidget(0,0, searchPanel);
var searchHeader = app.createFlexTable().setCellPadding(5);
searchPanel.add(searchHeader);
applyCSS_(searchHeader, _headerGrid);
```

Notice that there is CSS applied to the header table. This is the same CSS used to put a line under the search component and gives a nice consistency. Searching from the UI will now replace the welcome graphic with a tiny underline where the empty table is.

After the headers is the data, so make a second Flex Table to hold those and add it to the search panel. Because the search panel is a vertical panel, the two tables will line up nicely and appear to be the same table to the user.

```
var searchTable = app.createFlexTable().setId('searchTable');
searchPanel.add(searchTable);
```

Creating the Data Store

Now that there are a few tables, they need something to fill them but we don't have a data store yet. For this application we are going to use a Google Fusion Table (*http://www.google.com/fusiontables/public/tour/index.html#*). What is that? The short answer is a flat, non-relational database that can hold huge amounts of data. What makes it attractive is that it has many visualization tools built on top of it allowing you to see your data in very creative ways. For example, the application we are building in this chapter could have a location column that allows a direct export to Google Maps so you can see where your customers are being best served. Fusion Tables has an API, which is how we will connect to it. But what makes it a very interesting option for developers like you is that it uses SQL-style arguments to interact with the tables.

In Google Documents you can make a Fusion Table right from the Create button (Create→Table) or by going to: *https://www.google.com/fusiontables/showtables*.

Click "New Table" on the left and select "New empty table." You can change the name of the table (Edit→Modify table info), but what we are really interested in is the ID of the table. Look in the address bar and find the string after `dsrcid=`; that number is your table ID. *ᴵᴰ stops at char before &*

The Fusion Tables API will allow you to control the table by adding or removing columns, setting names and types of columns, and all the data access features you would expect. While you have the new table open, let's change around some of the columns so it will be set up for the application we are building in this chapter.

Click Edit, choose "Modify Table", and change the names and data types to match what you see in Figure 7-4.

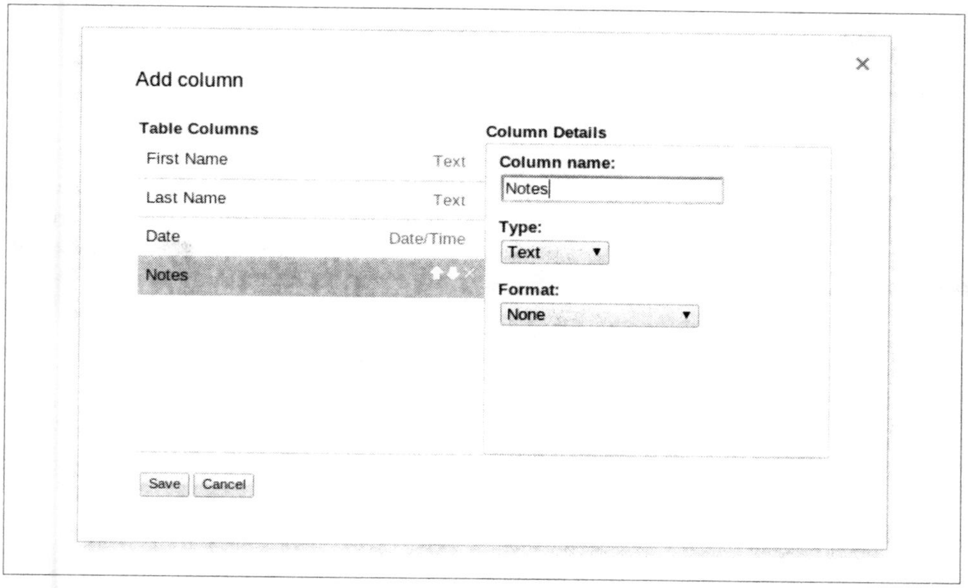

Figure 7-4. Fusion Tables use SQL statements, for example: sql=SELECT ROWID, Product, Inventory FROM 274409

If you make a mistake or need to delete/add a row, just go back to the Edit menu and find the choice to fix the problem.

Add a few rows of information to have something to work with while building the application. Once your columns are setup and a few records entered, make a note of the table ID and head back over to your script.

Importing Public Classes

The Fusion Tables API is easy to work with, but dealing with the authentication and translating your data from the UI to the SQL statement can be tedious to code. Good thing there is a public class to take care of all that for you.

Create a new file called **Fusion class** and then open the Fusion class source file at *http: //sites.google.com/site/scriptsexamples/custom-methods/fusion-tables-class/fusion -source*. Copy the source code and paste it in your "Fusion class" file.

Note that this class has some important instructions, namely the authentication type and table ID. The table ID needs to be put into a script property so that it can be changed at script runtime in the case that multiple tables are called. Open the Script Properties by clicking File➡Properties...➡Project properties➡Add row. Enter the property name as **FUSION_ID** and in the Value column, enter your Fusion Table ID, then click Save.

Script Properties has quota limits for the number of calls that can be made each day. At the time of this writing, this quota applies to all scripts under your account. You may need to code the table ID into your script if you are dealing with high call volumes.

```
var FUSION_ID = '1826800';
```

Choosing the authentication requires some thought about how your application will run. If you choose OAuth, you may need to come to the Script Editor and authenticate before the web interface will work. That's not much of a problem, the Fusion class has a doOAuth() method, which you should now run from the Script Editor. This will give you the typical grant access screens to click through. Run it a second time and check in the script log for a list of your tables. See one that looks familiar?

Keep in mind that all scripts in the UI run as you! Therefore anything you give your script access to will be accessible to those who can run the script.

The client side authentication method could allow for setting up a screen that requires the user to enter credentials, then you would need to process those in the app. We will be using the Oauth method.

If you read the instructions in the Fusion class, you would also note that it requires the GS Objects class. You used this class in Chapter 5; it is the same process to install as the Fusion class, however, there are no settings required.

Create a new file, name it **Objects class**, and copy and paste the source from *http://sites.google.com/site/scriptsexamples/custom-methods/gs-objects/source*. You won't need to come back to these files, so go ahead and close their tabs in the Editor.

Getting Data from a Fusion Table

After the Search button is clicked or the Enter key pressed, the script will need to know the value of the textBox. In the Search Component file, the name of the textBox was set to `searchbox` and can be called from the value passed from the handler in `e.parameter`.

```
var searchKey = e.parameter.searchBox;
```

The Fusion class has the method `searchFusion(target, where)`. The target specifies the columns you want to have returned in the search. It requires that each value be quoted. It can also take the all columns argument *. The only columns we want to search are first and last names, so we can trim down the list. The second argument is a SQL "WHERE" statement, which completes the query by saying: where the column named "First Name" contains your search key, return matching records but only the values in columns First Name and Last Name.

```
var arrayResult1 = searchFusion("'First Name', 'Last Name'", "'First Name'"+
                   " CONTAINS IGNORING CASE '"+ searchKey+"'");
```

We want to search both the first and last name, but there is not an "OR" to the "WHERE" statement, meaning a second call must be made:

```
var arrayResult2 = searchFusion("'First Name', 'Last Name'", "'Last Name'"+
                   " CONTAINS IGNORING CASE '"+ searchKey+"'");
```

The `searchFusion(target, where)` method returns an array `[[headers],[match row], [match row]...]`, which is perfect for turning into an object that we can then easily call on for values. The problem is we need to combine them and we only want the first set of headers located at `[0]` in each array. Taking care of this requires a few JavaScript tricks and the help of splice and concat:

```
arrayResult2.splice(0,1);
var concatArray = arrayResult1.concat(arrayResult2);
```

Splice off the first element in array number two and then glue the second array onto the first using concat. If you wanted to search more columns, just repeat the splice on each new array. Then, in concat, line up the arrays in the argument (`arrayResult2, arrayResult3, ...`).

The search array is put together and can be made into an object.

```
var fusionSearch = rangeToObjects(concatArray);
```

As discussed in Chapter 5, `rangeToObjects` turns the header values into camel so "First Name" becomes "firstName". It also makes an object that can be used as `fusion`

`Search[0].`firstName to get the result to be the First Name value of the first result returned.

Figure 7-5 shows the relationships between the arrays and objects created in the last several steps.

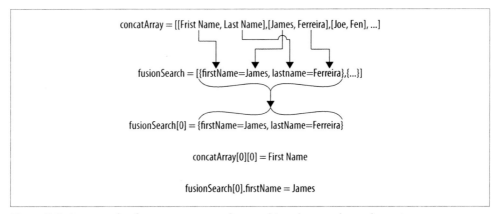

Figure 7-5. An example of an array converted to an object that uses key:value pairs

Loading the Data in the UI

The first element in the `concatArray` is an array of the column names, or the headers. When the search results are presented to the user they will need to know what the data is about and having headers will accomplish the task. Set up a `for` loop and iterate the first element in the `concatArray` using its bracket call `[0]`.

The `searchHeader` table will hold the header values going across the page, therefore, when you iterate, set each header value into its cell by using `parseInt(i)` in the table column. Note that you don't have to know what information was in the search above, the loop will take care of anything you hand to it.

Create a label widget to hold the value for each column, which is at `[0][i]`. Setting the width will help space things nicely across the application, but you may need to play with the value.

```
for (i in concatArray[0]){
  searchHeader.setWidget(0, parseInt(i), app.createLabel(concatArray[0][i])
                        .setWidth('150px'));
}
```

A few important points: you could use `setText` in place of `setWidget` and that would make for less coding, but it will also mean that you have less control over setting style properties for the headers.

What if you don't want to show certain columns? My question would be, "Why get them in the first place?" However, you might have a use case; let's look at that now.

Load the UI in the browser, type in a few letters that exist in one of the records added earlier, and see what you get. Figure 7-6 shows the headers have been returned from the Fusion Table telling us that everything is working up to this point and that there is an extra column, rowid, that we didn't ask for.

Figure 7-6. Using Labels for the headers gives better control over formatting.

In a Fusion Table, each row has a unique ID and is the only way to update a specific record. Therefore, having the row ID in your search results is important to working with a record, but you might not want that to show up for the user to see. To hide it from view, it needs to not load into the header table. Before the table loads a header value, inspect it to see if it has the name rowid; if it does, use the continue statement to have the loop skip to the next value:

```
if (concatArray[0][i]=='rowid')
    continue;
```

Now when you reload the page, it will only show the First and Last Name columns. To hide more columns add || (OR) statements to the loop conditions.

One reason for using the Fusion Class is that it adds the rowid that is not returned in a typical Fusion request. This simplifies working with the data.

The next step is to iterate through the results in the fusionSearch array and list out the values under each column. This could be done by simply adding the results into each row of the searchTable, however, the user should be able to click anywhere on the row and have that record open. If you add each value one at a time, you will also need to attach a click handler to each one. Later in this section there is a trick for highlighting the whole row that makes the upcoming solution even more attractive.

Remember a handler can be added to most widgets and the Flex Table will allow a click handler. We are going add a Flex Table to each row of the fusionSearch table, add a handler, and then fill the table in each row with the search results. Figure 7-7 shows the layout of tables in relation to the data they will hold.

For each element in the fusionSearch array, a new record table is created and a handler attached so that clicking anywhere in that row executes the viewRecord function. Most importantly each record table that is created will have an ID set to the rowid of the corresponding record that was returned in the search. When viewRecord runs, it will

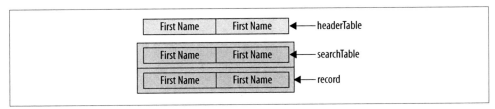

Figure 7-7. Example of flex tables within flex tables

look at `e.parameter.source` to see who called it; this is we will know which record was selected.

```
for(j in fusionSearch){
    var record = app.createFlexTable().setId(fusionSearch[j].rowid)
        .setCellPadding(5)
        .addClickHandler(app.createServerClickHandler('viewRecord'));
    applyCSS_(record, _rows);

//load record here

    searchTable.setWidget(parseInt(j), 0, record);
}
```

Additionally, CSS is applied to each row to add a line that separates each record. Don't forget to add a CSS entry in your CSS file.

```
var _rows =
    {
    "border-bottom":"2px solid #COCOCO"
    }
```

Find this text in the code: `//load record here`, and replace it with a loop to iterate the search results. This is done by iterating the number of headers in `concatArray[0]` as done above, giving "i" number of columns and also using the row in `fusion Search[j]`. To ensure the right value goes in the correct column, use `camelString(con catArray[0][i])`. Written in English, this would read, "Get the first header name and camel it, then find the matching value in the current row of data from the search results."

```
for (i in concatArray[0]){
    if (arrayResult1[0][i]=='rowid')
        continue;

    record.setWidget(parseInt(j), parseInt(i),
            app.createLabel(fusionSearch[j][camelString(concatArray[0][i])])
                        .setWidth('150px')
                // client Handlers go here
                        );
}
```

Again, the `rowid` is skipped over to hide it from the user.

At this point you can load the UI page, do a search, and see results. Clicking a row will throw an error, reminding you to create the add viewRecord function. There is something else amiss as well.

Adding Client Side Handlers

When you move the mouse over one of the records, nothing happens, so the user won't know if the item is selectable or even if they are hovering in the right place. The best way to give them feedback is to add a few mouse handlers to each record that will change the display. You might be wondering why we are adding these handlers to each label and not the Flex Table. The answer is that the Flex Table will not take a mouse handler, so we need a trick.

Unlike a standard handler that requires a trip to the server and back, the Client Side handlers run from the browser, giving a very fast response time. When the user rolls over one of the labels, the client handler will find the record with the right ID and change its text and background colors. Rolling off sets them back to the way they were. Now the user has positive feedback for the record they would like to select.

```
.addMouseOverHandler(app.createClientHandler()
  .forTargets(app.getElementById(fusionSearch[j].rowid))
    .setStyleAttribute('color', 'blue')
    .setStyleAttribute('background', 'FFFF99'))
.addMouseOutHandler(app.createClientHandler()
  .forTargets(app.getElementById(fusionSearch[j].rowid))
    .setStyleAttribute('color', 'black')
    .setStyleAttribute('background', 'transparent'))
```

Viewing a Record

The user can search for records in the database; the next step is to focus on one record to view all of the details. The process is very similar to displaying the search results, but the columns will be listed down the page with a label on the left and a text box on the right. Later certain headers will be picked out to allow special formatting, like a bigger box for the note field.

Figure 7-8 shows an example of how the layout will look using the columns in the example, however, the columns will be automatically generated to allow for changes in the database without the need to hardcode what will display.

The record view will replace the search results in the content screen, therefore it can be thought of as a component similar to the others.

Fetch the Correct Record

Create a new file, name it **Record View**, and start off with the component code as before:

```
function viewRecord(e) {
  var app = UiApp.getActiveApplication();
  //add code here
  return app;
}
```

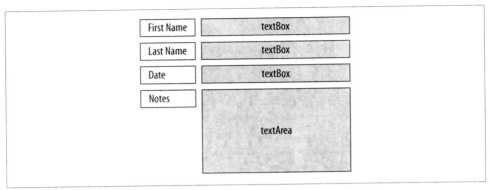

Figure 7-8. Example of flex tables within flex tables

If you remember back to the last section, each row in the `searchTable` was given the ID of the `rowid` from where the record came. This allows us to use `e.parameter.source` to find out the name of the called. Handy that the caller is the record ID that we need to display. Load the ID into a variable to make the code more readable and use the `search Fusion` method to call on a specific record:

```
var recordId = e.parameter.source;
var arrayResult = searchFusion("*", "'rowid' = '"+recordId+"'");
var fusionRecord = rangeToObjects(arrayResult)[0];
```

The arguments say that we want all `"*"` columns where the `'rowid'` is equal to the `recordId` variable. Because each row in a fusion table has a unique ID, there will be only one result. Next the values need to be paired with each column using the `rangeToOb jects` method. This returns an array even though it is only one element long. To save some writing, trim down the array to a single object using `[0]`.

Alright, the correct record has been retrieved and the values loaded into a workable format. To create the UI, we need a Flex Table to fill with the content from the database.

```
var viewRecordTable =
    app.createFlexTable().setCellPadding(5).setId('viewRecordTable');
    app.getElementById('contentGrid').setWidget(0,0, viewRecordTable);
```

 Unless you have some tricky arrangement for the panels and widgets, it's a good idea to get into the habit of adding them to their parent right after creating them. Even though we add the `viewRecordTable` to the `contentGrid` right after creating it, the table can be modified and more elements added to it later in the code.

The `arrayResult[0]` holds the column names from the database, for example, [`First Name`, `Last Name`, `Date`, `Notes`, `rowid`]. Don't forget that the `searchFusion` method always adds the `rowid`. To fill the `viewRecordTable` with content, iterate the values in `arrayResult[0]`.

There are two elements that need to be created: a label for the name of the column and a textBox to hold the value. The first element in the **setWidget** method will specify the row in the Flex Table and you must use **(parseInt(i)** to ensure that it has been turned into an integer. Flex Tables are zero-based so to put the label in the far left column, use the "0" argument for placing the label. Putting the textBox right next to the label is position "1". As discussed in Chapter 5, the elements were arranged three across the page and in rows continuing down the page for as much content in the database. If that is the look you are going for, a few more loops should get you there. Getting a specific look or arrangement is coming up in the next section.

```
for (var i in arrayResult[0]){

    viewRecordTable.setWidget(parseInt(i), 0, app.createLabel(arrayResult[0][i]));
    viewRecordTable.setWidget(parseInt(i), 1, app.createTextBox()
                    .setId(camelString(arrayResult[0][i]))
                    .setName(camelString(arrayResult[0][i]))
                    .setValue(fusionRecord[camelString(arrayResult[0][i])])
                    .setWidth('350px').setEnabled(false)
                );
}
```

Use the **arrayResult[0][i]** to get the column's name and create the label. For the text-Box, we want the ID and Name values to both be cameled text of the column name.

 Widget Name and ID values must be JavaScript safe or they will throw errors. The **camelString** method in the GS Object class (*http://sites.goo gle.com/site/scriptsexamples/custom-methods/gs-objects*) will make the conversion for you.

The value for the column is held in **fusionRecord.<columnName>**. To ensure you get the right value for the right column, call on the current column name being iterated and camel it.

A little increase on the width gives a better presentation and the textBox is set to disabled. The reason we set the textBox to disabled is to provide a View Only mode in the application. We don't want any changes unless they are intended, right?

Reload the UI page, do a search, and click one of the records. Figure 7-9 shows the specific record displayed in the content area, organized by rows.

Custom Formatting

Having all the details show up for the correct record is a great first step, but what if you need to hide something or make certain areas different than others? The **rowid** is not something your user will care about and that note field is too small to read longer entries. To solve these issues, we will need to create a way to check if a certain column is going to be loaded and perform the appropriate action.

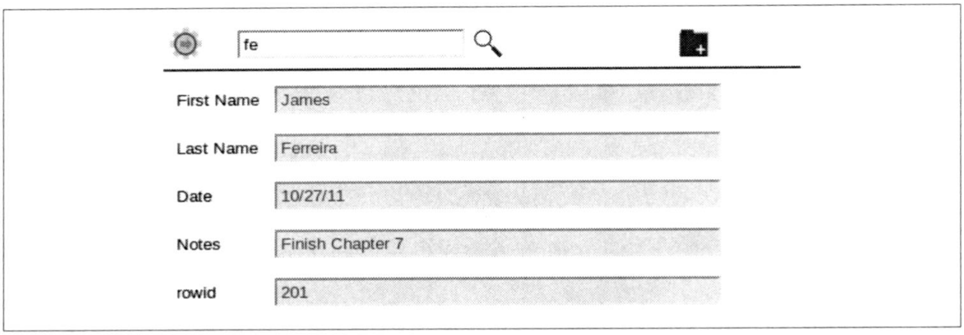

Figure 7-9. View record mode disables the text boxes to prevent unintended editing

One way to check the column is with an if/else if statement. Managing this gets messy and is not very efficient because each if statement must be evaluated before going to the next. This would not be a problem for our small database, but if your application was deployed in research, the number of columns could go into the thousands and that may make for a sluggish response.

In JavaScript, a better way to handle selecting specific criteria is to use a Switch statement. It works by giving it a value and then having it match cases (an optional default case will match if no cases fit the criteria).

Inside the for loop, modify the code to be set up as the default case. The value for the switch to evaluate is the column value. No need to camel it as each case can take a string value as its argument:

```
switch (arrayResult[0][i]){

    //add more cases here

    default:
      viewRecordTable.setWidget(parseInt(i), 0, app.createLabel(arrayResult[0][i]));
      viewRecordTable.setWidget(parseInt(i), 1, app.createTextBox()
                        .setId(camelString(arrayResult[0][i]))
                        .setName(camelString(arrayResult[0][i]))
                        .setValue(fusionRecord[camelString(arrayResult[0][i])])
                        .setWidth('350px').setEnabled(false)
                    );
    break;
}
```

To get started, the Notes section needs to be a text area not a box. This will give the user a larger area for display and scroll bars if the text goes beyond the size settings.

Insert the Notes case above the default case:

```
case 'Notes':
  viewRecordTable.setWidget(parseInt(i), 0, app.createLabel(arrayResult[0][i]));
  viewRecordTable.setWidget(parseInt(i), 1, app.createTextArea()
                    .setSize('350px', '100px')
                    .setId(camelString(arrayResult[0][i]))
```

```
                    .setName(camelString(arrayResult[0][i]))
                    .setValue(fusionRecord[camelString(arrayResult[0][i])])
                    .setEnabled(false)
                );
    break;
```

Each case starts with the column name as a quoted string and ends with break;. Change the textBox to .createTextArea() and use setSize to give the box some boundaries.

The rowid, while very important to the application, has no meaning to the user. Set a case for it and hide it by setting its visibility to false. Why load it at all? We will get to that when saving changes (think e.parameter).

```
case 'rowid':
  //No label required
  viewRecordTable.setWidget(parseInt(i), 1, app.createTextBox()
              .setId(camelString(arrayResult[0][i]))
              .setName(camelString(arrayResult[0][i]))
              .setValue(fusionRecord[camelString(arrayResult[0][i])])
              .setVisible(false) //hide the row
            );
  break;
```

Formatting a listBox

So far this application has displayed text, but it would be useful to have the user make a selection from a predefined list. The listBox is the widget that displays as a drop-down box with selections to choose from and can be created just like the text box but with a few more steps to set up the options.

Open your Settings file and create an array with the options you would like to appear in the list:

```
var statusValues = ['Open', 'Pending', 'Closed'];
```

Next open the Fusion table and add a new Status column: click Edit, add column, type in Status and the column name, and use the arrow icon to move it above the Notes column as shown in Figure 7-10.

If you reloaded the UI page, you would see the new Status column has to be generated as a text box.

The Status case is similar to the other cases but has additional code to add values to the listBox from the array in the Settings file. For a new record, the Status column will be an empty string and will render as a blank box with a down arrow. That will be fine for this application, but if you need to present more information to the user, simply add an if statement before the listBox is created to handle empty strings.

```
case 'Status':
  viewRecordTable.setWidget(parseInt(i), 0, app.createLabel(arrayResult[0][i]));
  var status = app.createListBox()
            .setId(camelString(arrayResult[0][i]))
            .setName(camelString(arrayResult[0][i]))
```

Figure 7-10. The format of the column is set in the type dropdown

```
                    .addItem(fusionRecord[camelString(arrayResult[0][i])])
                    .setWidth('100px').setEnabled(true);
    viewRecordTable.setWidget(parseInt(i), 1, status);

    for (k in statusValues){
        if (statusValues[k] != fusionRecord[camelString(arrayResult[0][i])])
        status.addItem(statusValues[k]);
    }
    break;
```

After creating the listBox, the for loop loads in the options from the array and includes a check for an existing value so it is not displayed twice in the list. Note that in the code above that the listBox is enabled so you can click on it. Don't bother disabling it because a variable will be added in the "Creating a New Record" section to control that.

Reload the UI page and go through the steps to set up a record. Now click the Status listBox and choose an option.

Edit a Record

Things are looking good. The user has an application that opens with a nice greeting, searches the database by entering key words, and displays specific records. We did not want to allow a record to be changed while viewing to avoid inadvertent changes and now the functionality will be added to make edits. This is actually very easy to do: simply enable the textBoxes. However, there will need to be a button and method to perform the task.

Open the Settings file and add an Edit icon:

```
var editIcon = 'https://sites.google.com/site/scriptsexamples/editIcon.png';
```

An Edit button is created before the `return app;` line and placed in position (0, 1) of the navPanel. It will call on the `editRecord` function, yet to be created and pass the `viewRecordTable` in the callback.

```
var editButton = app.createImage(editIcon)
    .setVisible(true)
    .setSize('25px', '25px')
    .setId('editButton')
    .addClickHandler(app.createServerClickHandler('editRecord')
                .addCallbackElement(viewRecordTable));
app.getElementById('navPanel').setWidget(0, 1, editButton);
```

Create a new file and name it **Edit Record**. Write the `editRecord` function and get/return the active application.

The Fusion Tables Class (*http://sites.google.com/site/scriptsexamples/custom-methods/fusion-tables-class*) has the `getFusionHeaders()` method, which returns an array of all the column names. Use camel array on this and you will have an array of column names that match the textBox names. Iterate the headers and set each matching element to enabled:

```
function editRecord(e){
  var app = UiApp.getActiveApplication();

  var headers = camelArray(getFusionHeaders());

  for (i in headers){
    app.getElementById(headers[i]).setEnabled(true);
  }

  app.getElementById('editButton').setVisible(false);
  app.getElementById('newFileButton').setVisible(false);

  return app;
}
```

During Edit mode, you don't want the user to create a new record; you are already editing, so hide these buttons by setting their visibility.

Save your work and reload the UI. The Edit button will appear when a record is loaded in View mode and clicking Edit will enable all the textBoxes.

There are two outcomes to editing a record: save the changes or cancel to not save changes. Let's deal with cancel first.

Open the View Record file and add a Cancel button after the Edit button. The visibility is set to false so the Cancel button is not seen when the view is loaded. The function it calls will be `viewRecord`. That is interesting because `viewRecord` was what loaded the View mode. What we are doing here is reloading the view for the same record without making changes, giving the appearance that the data was reset in the application.

```
var cancelButton = app.createImage(cancelIcon)
    .setVisible(false)
    .setSize('25px', '25px')
    .setId('cancelButton')
    .addClickHandler(app.createServerClickHandler('viewRecord')
                .addCallbackElement(viewRecordTable));
app.getElementById('navPanel').setWidget(0, 3, cancelButton);
```

Don't forget to add a cancel icon in the Settings file:

```
var cancelIcon = 'https://sites.google.com/site/scriptsexamples/CancelIcon.png';
```

To make the button show up in the navigation, add a line at the end of the Edit Record file to make it visible:

```
app.getElementById('cancelButton').setVisible(true);
```

If you tried the Cancel button now it would give you an error because when `viewRecord` runs, it uses the name of the caller to find the record. Coming from the search, the name is a `rowid`, but coming from the Cancel button, the name is `e.parameter.source` = `cancelButton`. At first this appears to be a huge problem, but remember that `viewRecordTable` was passed in the cancel handler and that `e.parameter.rowid` holds the `rowid` value. See why we just hid it earlier?

To make the Cancel button work, modify the beginning of the View Record file to check `e.parameter.source` by replacing the line:

```
var recordId = e.parameter.source;
```

with an `if/else` statement to check if the Cancel button was clicked:

```
if (e.parameter.source == 'cancelButton'){
  var recordId = e.parameter.rowid;
  app.getElementById('newFileButton').setVisible(true);
}else{
  var recordId = e.parameter.source;
}
```

Reload the UI page and check the operation. When changes like deleting content are made, clicking Cancel resets the record and places the user back in View Only mode.

Save Changes

When the user makes changes, these changes will need to be written to the spreadsheet. First create a Save button. As with the Cancel button, an icon is added to the navigation panel.

 In this chapter, icons have been used for the buttons to create a custom look and feel. However, if you don't have the time or don't care to take the time, use a button widget. By using CSS to style all the buttons, you can add a creative flair with rounded corners and other effects.

In the Settings file add a save icon:

```
var saveIcon = 'https://sites.google.com/site/scriptsexamples/saveicon.png';
```

Insert the Save button in the Record View file after the Cancel button so it can join its friends in the navPanel at location (0,2). The arrangement between the buttons is not really important, just don't put two buttons in the same cell or only the second one set will show, making for a great deal of confusion and troubleshooting. The handler will execute the saveRecord function that has not been created and, like the Cancel button, it adds the viewRecordTable as the callback, giving access to all the widgets contained in the table.

```
var saveButton = app.createImage(saveIcon)
    .setVisible(false)
    .setSize('25px', '25px')
    .setId('saveButton')
    .addClickHandler(app.createServerClickHandler('saveRecord')
                    .addCallbackElement(viewRecordTable));
app.getElementById('navPanel').setWidget(0,2, saveButton);
```

You will need to change the visibility of the Save button in the Edit Record file when the edit view is loaded by adding one more line before returning the app:

```
app.getElementById('saveButton').setVisible(true);
```

The buttons are now in order and the Save Record file can be created to handle saving to the Fusion table. What it takes to save to the Fusion table may surprise you:

```
function saveRecord(e){
    var app = UiApp.getActiveApplication();

    writeFusionObj(e.parameter);

    return app;
}
```

I'm joking, it is only one line of code. The reason is that the Fusion Tables Class method —writeFusionObj—uses the values in e.parameter to determine which row needs to be written to and the correct values for each column.

The user should be notified that the changes were saved and the best way to do that is the "Last look" scenario: send them back to the View Only mode after the save, where they can check the values are correct before leaving.

The values are already there in the textBoxes, so disable them and update the visibility of the buttons:

```
for (i in headers){
    app.getElementById(headers[i]).setEnabled(false);
}

app.getElementById('cancelButton').setVisible(false);
app.getElementById('saveButton').setVisible(false);
app.getElementById('newFileButton').setVisible(true);
app.getElementById('editButton').setVisible(true);
```

Insert a New Record

It may have seemed strange to wait until so late in the application development to start creating new records, but this is because inserting a record is more of a piggyback on the work that is already done and there is no need to add any new files.

The button has been hanging around in the navigation bar forever, so it is time to put it to work. Looking back to the Navigation Component where the button was first created, you will note that it executes the `viewRecord` function. If you are having déja vu, don't worry, you ran into the same problem with the Cancel button.

Open the Record View file and get ready to make a few changes. When the `viewRecord` runs, all the textBoxes are disabled and that would mean an extra click to start entering data. To overcome this limitation, create a variable for enabled status right after the app is created and replace the three false values in the `setEnabled` calls to `newRecord`. Right now that will have the exact same effect, but it gives us the option to toggle `newRecord` to true and have all the textBoxes live when loading `viewRecord`.

```
var newRecord = false;
```

Reading down the code, skip past the `if` statement for the Cancel button and create a new `if` statement to handle the `newFileButton`. The `e.parameter.source` will tell us that the caller is the `newFileButton`. The idea is to create an object that is the same as what would be created by running a search for a specific ID but with empty values. Grab the column names with the `getFusionHeaders` method. You will need to add `rowid` by pushing it into the `arrayHeaders`. To work in the rest of the code, `arrayHeaders` needs to be enclosed in brackets and set as the value for `arrayResult`. The `fusionRecord` can be an empty object because we don't want any values. This is a new record so set `newRecord = true`.

To preserve the previous function, add an `else` statement and enclose the two lines that created the data variables:

```
if (e.parameter.source == 'newFileButton'){
  var arrayheaders = getFusionHeaders();
  arrayheaders.push('rowid');
  var arrayResult = [arrayheaders]
  var fusionRecord = new Object();
  newRecord = true;
}else{
  var arrayResult = searchFusion("*", "'rowid' = '"+recordId+"'");
  var fusionRecord = rangeToObjects(arrayResult)[0];
}
```

Because the UI is going to load with the textBoxes enabled there is no need for the Edit button to be showing. To hide it, go to the end of the code before the app returns and add an `if` statement to check for the `newRecord` value and hide the Edit button if true:

```
if(newRecord)
  editButton.setVisible(false);
```

Reloading the UI page and clicking the Create Record button will now load the form ready to accept values as shown in Figure 7-11.

Figure 7-11. *The Create Record form is the same as the Edit form but no record has been inserted*

Inserting a record in a Fusion Table is not the same call as saving a record and requires a different method. Currently there is no value in the rowid and that could be detected from a Save button press, however, to add some distinction for the user, an Insert Record button will be used.

You know the drill, add an icon in the Settings file:

```
var insertIcon = 'https://sites.google.com/site/scriptsexamples/
InsertRecordIcon.png';
```

Add an Insert button at the end of the other buttons in the Record View file:

```
var insertRecordButton = app.createImage(insertIcon)
    .setVisible(newRecord)
    .setSize('25px', '25px')
    .setId('insertRecordButton')
    .addClickHandler(app.createServerClickHandler('saveRecord')
                    .addCallbackElement(viewRecordTable));
app.getElementById('navPanel').setWidget(0,4, insertRecordButton);
```

This will give the user a different look to inserting over saving.

Moving over to the Save Record file, add an if statement to detect the insertRecord Button press. The insertFusionObj method returns the rowid for the inserted row and calling it within the setValue method will set the value into the UI all at the same time. It looks a bit tricky but is an easy way to combine functions. Wrap up the writeFusio nObj call in an else statement to keep the Save button working:

```
if(e.parameter.source == 'insertRecordButton'){
  app.getElementById('rowid')
    .setValue(insertFusionObj(e.parameter).toString())
    .setEnabled(false);
```

```
  }else{
    writeFusionObj(e.parameter);
  }
```

After the Insert button has been pressed, the user will be returned to View mode. This means the Insert button needs to be hidden before returning the app:

```
app.getElementById('insertRecordButton').setVisible(false);
```

Reload the UI page and create a record. After inserting the record, do a search and you will see the new record in the search results.

Deleting a Record

At this point you could probably guess how to delete a record, but we will go through the steps one last time so your application is polished and ready to deploy.

Back in the Settings file, add a delete icon:

```
var deleteIcon = 'https://sites.google.com/site/scriptsexamples/killRecord.png';
```

In the Record View file, add the Delete button after the others and set the handler to execute the deleteRecord function:

```
var deleteButton = app.createImage(deleteIcon)
    .setVisible(false)
    .setSize('25px', '25px')
    .setId('deleteButton')
    .addClickHandler(app.createServerClickHandler('deleteRecord')
                    .addCallbackElement(viewRecordTable));
app.getElementById('navPanel').setWidget(0,5, deleteButton);
```

After saving a file the delete icon needs to be switched off; that happens at the end of the Save Record file:

```
app.getElementById('deleteButton').setVisible(false);
```

UI details out of the way, create a new Delete Record file and add a delete call to the Fusion Table. The UI will need to be updated with a message that the removal has taken place and buttons reset to the beginning state.

```
function deleteRecord(e){
    var app = UiApp.getActiveApplication();

    deleteFusionRow(e.parameter.rowid);

    app.getElementById('contentGrid')
       .setWidget(0,0, app.createLabel('Record has been Deleted forever!'));

    app.getElementById('cancelButton').setVisible(false);
    app.getElementById('saveButton').setVisible(false);
    app.getElementById('newFileButton').setVisible(true);
    app.getElementById('deleteButton').setVisible(false);
```

```
    return app;
}
```

The application is done; take a deep breath. As a final test, reload the UI page and create a new record. Do a search for the record and press the Edit button. Add some more information and click Save. Edit again and click Delete.

Where you go from here is a matter of customization from the core functionality you have built in this chapter.

Notes!

My App Needs Fixing
✓ • Delete Record Icon remove from New Record
✓ • Going Back to Search view - Remove all but New Record Icon
  • why is "Undefined" in all New Record fields?
→ • why can't you save when field has ' in it ex Billy's
✓ • ~~after~~ after Save put in Read Only mode
✓ • Remove Edit icon After Delete Record
→ • Similar issues w/ " character
✓ • Put Delete icon afte Ensert Record
✓ • Put some sort of Abort on The Insert Record
     Screen that take you Back to the Search View?
              used X cancel Icon
  • What about ";" comma?
  • Similar w/ Return char.

CHAPTER 8
Workflows

Back in the day, circa 2007, I was working at the New Mexico Office of Attorney General attempting to streamline the legislative bill analyses we performed each year. It was a crazy time for the office with more than a 1,000 bills going through the office in 30 days, legislators calling to get the latest update, and politics galore. Honestly, to this day, I'm baffled by how it all gets done while keeping the mortality rate so low.

The process starts with a legislator submitting a bill for analysis. The bill is assigned to different attorneys, depending on their area of practice, who write an analysis and send it off to reviewers that may send it to others who make edits and sent it back or to someone else and so on until the final approval where the analysis is sent back to the legislator. That sounds simple enough, but add a 24-hour deadline and politically charged issues; it is a recipe for a heart attack. Adding to the mayhem, the team at the legislative building and the upper management never knew what was being analyzed or where in the queue something might be. Not the best place to be when the chairman is fuming about a delay.

At the time, I thought we could add in a little technology to smooth out the flow of work and wouldn't you know it, we had just installed Sharepoint. It had workflows that we hoped to leverage into an email approval and tracking system. After a few weeks we eked out a rudimentary system that sort of worked most of the time. It was a painful learning curve and not very flexible in what we could do. Once a workflow started, it had to go through until it was done and could not be changed. It only worked in the office and not at all from the BlackBerrys. When we finally rolled it out, several early failures caused the staff that would use it to lose interest and they fell back to the old way of doing things. Epic project failure.

The good news is that times have changed and so have the tools available to handle workflows.

Building a Modern Email Workflow

Google Documents and Gmail are powerful tools for creation and collaboration, but they don't do workflow in the sense that a series of steps are tracked and completed by different people. This is where Google Script can come in and bridge the gap.

These days people are busy and on the go; they can't be expected to hang out at their desks all day waiting for something to hit their inbox so a certain installed program can be used to enter something. Google Docs works on everything, virtually anywhere, and that is what makes it such a powerful tool. Why shouldn't your workflow system be integrated and take advantage of Google Apps?

In this chapter, you will create a workflow builder that has a flexible nature so that it will fit many situations and can be customized on the fly by the user without any coding on their part. It will take advantage of Google Documents for file management, Gmail for notifications, and the Google Script UiApp to give users an interface. The application is robust, meaning workflows can be moved, restarted, redirected, steps added during runtime, parallel approvers, and other great workflow features.

What You Will Learn

You will learn about:

- Client side handlers
- Using a namespace
- Gmail integration
- Accessing Google Documents
- Advanced Flex Table interaction
- Dynamic event handlers
- Using the published URL to pass script values

Supplies

You will need:

- A Google Account
- A good grasp on the concepts and terminology used in Part I

Application Overview

The application will be launched from a link on a site or in an email. It should automatically detect if it needs to create a new workflow and present the user with a blank workflow. Information such as title and creator are entered and a Google Documents folder is added. Next, steps with approvers are added.

When the workflow is started, an email is sent to the person or people in the first step. They are presented with details and a link to access the workflow UI (See Figure 8-1). Approve and Reject buttons show for the current step, allowing the approver to decide what happens next. If they feel the next step is wrong, they can add a step right then. The whole process has structure but is also flexible because the world is unpredictable and your workflow application needs to be ready for that.

Our process will terminate with the completion of all the steps but suggestions will be made throughout the chapter on uses such as publishing a document to a public website after approval or emailing the final documents in a document review like described in the opening of this chapter.

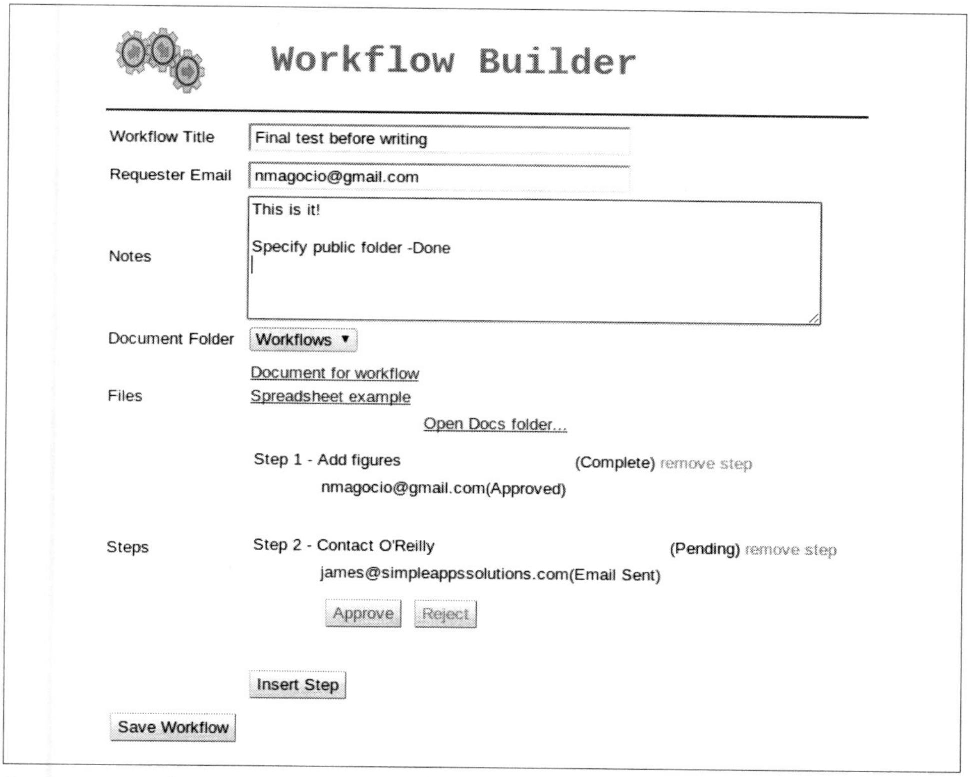

Figure 8-1. Simple yet powerful, a good workflow can smooth out the bumps of the workday.

Using a Namespace

Let's dive in.

This is not a huge script in terms of lines of code, but because it is quite complex, the concept of namespace will be introduced. This does lead to more typing, but it will make the code infinitely easier to understand.

Open a new spreadsheet and create a script. This example will use a spreadsheet to store the workflow information but could be easily adapted to use a different data storage like Fusion Tables as shown in Chapter 7.

In the new script, create a file and name it **Namespace**. Because JavaScript is a top down language, it is important that this be the first file created. Add this code:

```
var FILE = FILE || {};
```

This will create a FILE object that will become the parent for the namespace. As more files are created and global variables added, they will be added to the namespace, making them easy to find. For example, you are reading through a 2,000 line doGet file in a script with 10 files, all with hundreds of lines of code. You see the function getSometh ing(); how will you know where that function is? It could be anywhere and you may spend 15 minutes trying to find it; not a very efficient use of your time. Using a namespace, the same function may look like FILE.utilities.getSomething(), telling you that the function is located in the utilities file.

To put namespace into practice, create another file named **CSS**. The first line defines the file css in the namespace of FILE. As global variables, meaning anything that will be called from another file, are added to the css file, they are placed inside the namespace.

```
FILE.css = {};

    FILE.css.setStyle = function(element, style){
       for (var key in style){
          element.setStyleAttribute(key, style[key]);
        }
      }

    FILE.css.headerGrid =
       {
       "border-bottom":"2px solid #404040"
       }

    FILE.css.rows =
       {
       "border-bottom":"2px solid #C0C0C0"
       }

    FILE.css.header =
       {
       "color": "#37F",
       "font": "bold 30px Courier New, Courier, monospace"
       }

    FILE.css.submitTy =
       {
```

```
"font": "bold 18px Courier New, Courier, monospace",
"text-indent":"20px"
}
```

This script uses the public Workflow Class to help simplify the amount of code you need to write. Create a file and name it **Workflow Class**. Copy the Workflow Class (*https://sites.google.com/site/scriptsexamples/custom-methods/workflow/workflow -source*) and paste it into the new file. This will allow you to create workflow objects that contain constructors for the common use case.

For example:

```
var workflow = new Workflow();
workflow.setTitle('Your New Workflow');
```

That should do it for the basics, now it's time to get down to business and build the first part of the UI.

Building the UI

Workflows come in many flavors: some are entirely done through email, others send email notices and have a web interface, and still others are application specific and do not communicate outside at all. The Workflow application in this chapter takes the middle road, a web page UI for building and manage the workflows and a notification system to send emails. The two systems are tightly integrated but notifications will be bolted on after getting the manager is complete.

Create a new file called **doGet** and add it to the namespace:

```
FILE.doGet = {};
```

Next add the basic parts of a UI:

```
function doGet(e) {
  var app = UiApp.createApplication().setTitle('Workflow Builder');
  //code goes here
  return app;
}
```

Open the Share menu, publish the script, and get the published URL. You can open a new page with the published URL to test out development as we move along.

Application Layout

This application is dynamic in nature as items will be added or removed from the UI by pressing buttons or clicking links. The UI itself will also load differently depending on parameters passed in the published URL.

Keep in mind that your UI doesn't need to look anything like what you see here. This is a starting point that establishes the functionality and by all means, go crazy adding CSS beauty. Do keep in mind that when a grid or table is specified, it is likely because something later on will be calling on a specific cell. Adjust accordingly.

Figure 8-2 shows the layout of the grids required to hold the content. The `mainGrid` is two rows by one column and is the parent of all the other elements. This layout works well for providing a banner area at the top of the page with content filling the cell below.

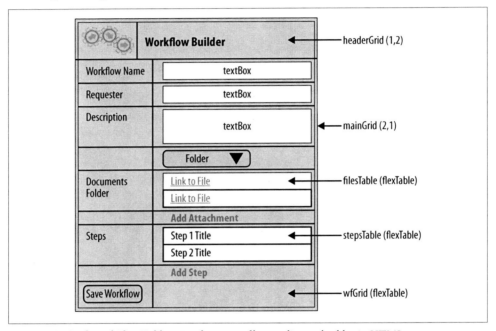

Figure 8-2. Grids and Flex Tables give the same effect as divs and tables in HTML

The mainGrid will be called on by many operations throughout the script but not in a global variable fashion. To update the mainGrid it will be passed through a handler and accessed using `getElementById`. Following along in the namespace scheme, use `FILE_doGet_elementName` to identify it by the namespace.

```
var mainGrid = app.createGrid(2,1).setId('FILE_doGet_mainGrid');
app.add(mainGrid);
```

The header is a (1,2) grid that holds a logo in the first cell and the application title in the next. Insert this grid into cell (0,0) of the `mainGrid` to form two columns in the top cell. Adding some CSS will give a nice line to separate the header from the content. Here you see the first example of using the namespace to call on a function and variable from another file.

```
var headerGrid = app.createGrid(1,2).setWidth('600px');
mainGrid.setWidget(0,0, headerGrid);
FILE.css.setStyle(headerGrid, FILE.css.headerGrid);
```

What would an application be without a logo? As in the other chapters, branding should be controlled in a Settings file so it is easy to redistribute your application. Create a **Settings** file and add a link to a logo that works well for the space. The image gets sized back in the doGet file so an image that is sort of square should do fine. While you are here in the Settings file, it is a good time to collect some other information that will be needed later.

The workflows will be saved in a spreadsheet and use `SpreadsheetApp.openById` for access. Put the ID here so it is easy to change if you copy the script. Same goes for the UiApp published URL, which we will need for sending approval links in emails.

```
FILE.settings = {};

  FILE.settings.logo = 'https://sites.google.com/site/scriptsexamples/
WorkflowLogo.png';
  FILE.settings.ssId = 'OAq1-C9Nl4dO-dG9ZUWZJN2RlLTI1UG1ISlIyWGkxdHc';

  FILE.settings.publishedUrl = 'https://docs.google.com/a/macros/
simpleappssolutions.com/'+
      'exec?service=AKfycbxQHhK-QjTROF9089RFVspf-5T5FXChWFOQMm58';
```

Back in the doGet file, an image is created from the link in Settings and added to the header along with the title of the application. CSS style is applied to the `headerTitle` text giving it a custom look:

```
    headerGrid.setWidget(0, 0, app.createImage(FILE.settings.logo).setSize('75px',
'75px'));
    var headerTitle = app.createLabel('Workflow Builder');
    headerGrid.setWidget(0, 1, headerTitle);
    FILE.css.setStyle(headerTitle, FILE.css.header);
```

The content area holds several elements (refer to Figure 8-2) and needs to be updated by the script. A flexTable is a perfect option for this case.

```
    var wfGrid = app.createFlexTable().setId('FILE_doGet_wfGrid')
    mainGrid.setWidget(1,0, wfGrid);
```

That rounds out the structure of the application and gives us a foundation to build on.

Entering the Application

Users from all over your organization will be making workflows to help them through their day; to access the Workflow Builder, they will use a link on the corporate website or one you distribute in an email. The link text should say something like *Create Work flow*. When the link is clicked, the UI will begin to load and the first thing to decide is if the UI should load a new workflow or one that already exists.

When you need input for the UI to load, pass the information using URL parameters. This is done by adding &parameter=value to the end of the published UiApp URL. These parameters show up in the doGet(e) arguments as e.parameter.*parameter*. A unique ID will be assigned to each workflow when they are created, making them easy to find later. This means that passing the workflow ID in the URL will tell the UI what to load. Conversely, if the parameter does not exist in the URL, an undefined value is returned when trying to access it.

The parameter will be called wfId and looks like this in the URL:

```
http://<published_URL>&wfId=<uniqueId>
```

An if statement will look at e.paramerter.wfId for an undefined value and load a new workflow if true. If there is a value for wfId it can be assumed that an ID must also exist.

```
if(e.parameter.wfId == undefined){

    //Create new workflow

}else{

    //Load existing workflow

}
```

Creating a New Workflow

If the published UI is loaded without a wfId, we will assume the user has clicked the Create Workflow link. The first step in creating a new workflow is to make a new workflow object from the Workflow Class. This goes inside the if part of the e.param eter.wfId check.

```
var workflow = new Workflow();
```

The next step is to give it an ID. There are many ways to create a unique ID such as using the exact time in milliseconds, but for this example we will create a random ID generator. After the closing bracket of the doGet function add the following:

```
FILE.doGet.randomString function() {
    var chars = "0123456789ABCDEFGHIJKLMNOPQRSTUVWXTZabcdefghiklmnopqrstuvwxyz";
    var string_length = 10;
    var randomstring = '';
    for (var i=0; i<string_length; i++) {
        var rnum = Math.floor(Math.random() * chars.length);
        randomstring += chars.substring(rnum,rnum+1);
    }
    return randomstring;
}
```

This function returns a 10-character string of upper- and lowercase letters and numbers (for example, s6Ih9Cd8tB). With 10 characters, the odds of getting two identical IDs is quite unlikely as in $8.39299366 \times 10^{17}$ to 1, but the more you play the better your chances.

Below the new workflow create the unique ID:

```
var wfId = FILE.doGet.randomString();
```

In order to access the workflow from other functions in the script, it will need to be saved to the spreadsheet. Start by getting the sheet using its ID from the Settings file and then the first empty row, which is the last row of data plus one. Now set the values into the correct columns: ID, Status, Workflow.

```
var ss = SpreadsheetApp.openById(FILE.settings.ssId).getSheets()[0];
var row = ss.getLastRow()+1;
ss.getRange(row,1,1,3).setValues([[wfId, 'New', JSON.stringify(workflow)]]);
```

 JSON.stringify is used whenever you need to save an object to a string while preserving its properties. This greatly cuts down on the number of cells needed to store information and allows for the preservation of complex relations in your spreadsheet or table-based storage.

That is all there is to creating a new workflow, next we will load an existing one.

Loading Workflows

To load an existing workflow, you need to know the wfId. This will normally be passed to the user via email or as a link on a page. You get the wfId from the URL using e.parameter.wfId; while you are at it, get the email parameter as well. These go in the else part of the if statement.

```
var wfId = e.parameter.wfId;
var email = e.parameter.email;
```

Now that you have the workflow ID, you will need to retrieve the workflow string from the spreadsheet and reloaded into a workflow as an object. This is a several step process and is best handled by a function that will simply return the workflow.

Create a new file, name it **SS Ops**, and add its namespace:

```
FILE.ssOps = {};
```

There are two operations that require you to write or read from the spreadsheet. Insert the following functions:

```
FILE.ssOps = {};

/*
*   @args:      wfId  String  id for a specific record
*   @returns:         Array   row from SS [wfId, status, workflow]
*
*/
FILE.ssOps.getWfRowFromSS = function(wfId) {
```

```
                var ss = SpreadsheetApp.openById(FILE.settings.ssId).getSheets()[0];
                var values = ss.getDataRange().getValues();
                for(i in values){
                  if(wfId == values[i][0]){
                    return values[i];
                    break;
                  }
                }
              }

              /*
               * @args: wfRowArray  Array  [wfId, status, workflow]
               */
              FILE.ssOps.setWftoSS = function(wfRowArray){
                var ss = SpreadsheetApp.openById(FILE.settings.ssId).getSheets()[0];
                var values = ss.getDataRange().getValues();
                for(i in values){
                  if(wfRowArray[0] == values[i][0]){
                    ss.getRange(parseInt(i)+1,1,1,3).setValues([wfRowArray]);
                    break;
                  }
                }
              }
```

Take a moment to read the comments. `FILE.ssOps.getWfRowFromSS` takes a workflow ID, looks in the spreadsheet for a match, and returns the row containing a match as an array. The second, `File.ssOps.setWftoSS`, takes an array like what is returned in the first function, finds the matching ID, and saves the arguments.

Go back to the `else` section in doGet and load the workflow like this:

```
              var wfRowArray = FILE.ssOps.getWfRowFromSS(wfId);
```

Remember that the workflow is still a string because it came from the spreadsheet and will need to be converted back to an object using `ReLoadJson` from the Workflow Class.

```
              var jsonText = wfRowArray[2];
              var workflow = ReLoadJson(jsonText);
```

`If/else` is done and depending on whether the `wfId` was passed in the URL, you have either a new workflow or one that was already created. If you reload the published page, the UI will look the same, but you will not see that there is a new row in the spreadsheet. Adding `&wfId=YourWfId` and reloading again will not create a new workflow but rather load the one you entered the ID for, which is empty at the moment.

Displaying the Workflow Details

Now that the correct workflow is ready, we can start putting together a form for the top half of the UI. The `wfGrid` is used and filled with the information from a workflow object. This is a standard form layout with the label going into column 0 and text boxes in column 1. The values for the text boxes come from the workflow object for that certain field (for example: `workflow.getTitle()`). Calling on a workflow parameter that has not been set, like what you have right now, will simply return an empty string appearing as a blank field. Set the name property for each text box and change the size to better fit the space of the application; refer back to Figure 8-2 to get an idea of how the elements should look on the page.

```
wfGrid.setWidget(0,0, app.createLabel('Workflow Title'));
wfGrid.setWidget(0,1, app.createTextBox()
                .setName('wfTitle')
                .setWidth('300px')
                .setValue(workflow.getTitle()));

wfGrid.setWidget(1,0, app.createLabel('Requester Email'));
wfGrid.setWidget(1,1, app.createTextBox()
                .setName('wfRequester')
                .setWidth('300px')
                .setValue(workflow.getRequester()));

wfGrid.setWidget(2,0, app.createLabel('Notes'));
wfGrid.setWidget(2,1, app.createTextArea()
                .setName('wfNote')
                .setSize('450px','100px')
                .setValue(workflow.getNote()));
//Add Docs

//Add Steps

//Hide some values

//Save the workflow
```

Accessing Google Documents

Most of the time your workflows are going to have to do with some operation that has supporting documents or other events that go along with it. The purchase request is an example where there may be several documents: the quote from the vendor, a company request for the issued purchase order, and an invoice when the product arrives. There are many solutions to attaching documents to a workflow such as using the file upload widget, or the Workflow Attachments Class. However, the user will need to get the files online and that means we would need to handle many variables.

It is my hope that more of the process of document management will move to solutions like Google Documents, which offers many options for dealing with documents. For example, if the document is attached to your workflow from a website, somewhere you have added a second layer of management process like revision tracking and such. This is all built into Google Documents so we can save considerable time by simply extending that platform to interact with ours.

The method we will use assumes that if you are going to have a workflow that contains documents then it should allow those involved with the workflow to add, view, and edit the documents as you, the workflow creator, determines. To accomplish the task, the UI will load a Google Documents collection specified in a list box on the UI. This will allow you to easily change the collection from workflow to workflow.

 Remember that the UiApp runs as you and if you tell it to list all the collections in your account and the files in those collections, it will happily complete that task. That does not mean the files can be opened—the sharing security still exists—but the details you allow the UI to display will be given to anyone who has access to the script.

For security, it is a good idea to only give your script access to a specific collection in your Google Documents and then add collections inside that collection for the access level you think is appropriate. This will give you the ability to share certain documents with view or edit permissions without having to manage that in the workflow itself. A further advantage happens when a step and approver gets added along the line that you did not anticipate if you may or may not have wanted them to see the documents. If they do attempt to open a document they have not been given access to, they will get a screen prompting them to contact you for access.

To reduce access to your collections, open your Google Documents list and create a collection called **Public**. In the Public collection, create another collection called **Workflow 1** and inside that collection add some files. Share access to the Workflow 1 collection or the files within to those involved in your workflow. An alternative is to not share access and let them request it later. Those are choices you can make at any time.

Click on the Public collection so that its contents are displayed in the center, see Figure 8-3.

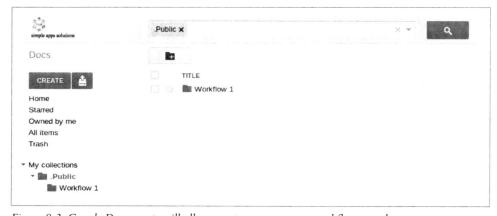

Figure 8-3. Google Documents will allow you to manage your workflow attachments.

Now get the collection ID from the address box in the browser. It is the long string following: `?tab=mo#folders/`.

Create a new variable in the Settings file containing the collection ID:

```
FILE.settings.publicCollectionId = 'Your_ID_Goes_Here';
```

The Workflow Documents Folder Class will be used to store the collection details so that they can be reloaded with the workflow. This class returns an array of folders, but for this application we will only use one folder.

When the UI loads, we want the application to get the right collection and display the files inside. The list box that allows you to choose the collection should also display the name of the collection and have a list of other folders available in the public collection. The problem is, if a collection has not been set in the workflow, getting the array from the workflow will return undefined, which throws an errors if you try to load it as a value in the list box. Figure 8-4 shows a flowchart explaining the different gates that are passed to load files in the UI.

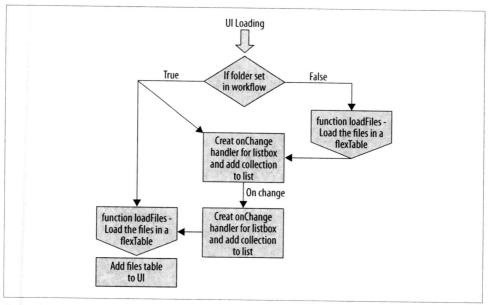

Figure 8-4. Getting updates to the UI on load

To avoid an error and give the user better feedback, we will check to see if a collection exists in the workflow; if not, we'll create a notification for the user. If a folder already exists, then run the FILES.docs.loadFiles function. We will look at this function in just a minute, but for now know that it returns a Flex Table filed with the names of each file in the current collection at workflow.getDocsFolders()[0].

```
if(workflow.getDocsFolders()[0] == undefined){
  workflow.addDocsFolder().setName('Please select folder');
}else{
  wfGrid.setWidget(4,1, FILES.docs.loadFiles(app, workflow.getDocsFolders()
```

```
[0].getId()));
    }
```

As the code reads down, let's assume that a folder did not exist and we have skipped over loading any files in the UI list. The next part of the code will add the list box for choosing a collection.

Set the name and ID so the list box can be accessed through server handlers. Next add the collection name stored in (`workflow.getDocsFolders()[0].getName()`. If this is a new workflow, the `if` statement above tells us that the folder name is "Please select folder". Nothing special needs to be done to load a collection name as it will be stored in the same workflow parameter. I know this may seem a little tricky, but it gives us an effective way to ensure the user gets the right choice displayed in the list box when it loads.

```
wfGrid.setWidget(3,0, app.createLabel('Document Folder'));
var docsFolder = app.createListBox()
                .setName('docsFolder').setId('docsFolder')
                .addItem(workflow.getDocsFolders()[0].getName())
    .addChangeHandler(app.createServerChangeHandler('FILE_docs_loadDocs')
                .addCallbackElement(mainGrid));
```

You might be wondering why we use a function to load the files list instead of just loading them in doGet. Remember that the UiApp must return to the browser to refresh the display. If we load the files directly that would mean adding additional code to replace the list if the user changes the collection in the listbox, and we don't like to rewrite the same line of code twice.

Moving on to the list box handler, we want the list to change each time a new selection is made so `addChangeHandler` is used. This is going to fire the function `FILE_docs_load Docs`. You might be wondering why that function is not part of the namespace, this is a limitation in Google Script and it means you will need to use a global function. The idea comes through with not much effort by replacing the periods with underscores. It is important to add the `mainGrid` as the callback, giving you access to the whole UI and specifically the `wfGrid`.

The next step is to load the list box with choices in the Public folder. Use `DocsList.get FolderById` and the ID you save in the variable `FILE.settings.publicCollectionId`. Next, iterate the folders array and add each one by name to the list box.

Finish up by adding the list box to the `wfGrid` along with a label for the files:

```
var folders = DocsList.getFolderById(FILE.settings.publicCollectionId)
                    .getFolders();
for(i in folders){
  docsFolder.addItem(folders[i].getName());
}
wfGrid.setWidget(3,1, docsFolder);
wfGrid.setWidget(4,0, app.createLabel('Files'));
```

The stage is set, so reload the published URL. Now you have a list box ready to choose a Docs collection containing the files for your workflow.

If you see the error "Authorization is required to perform that action" when loading the published URL, it is because a service requires you give it authorization. Go to the Script Editor and click Run. You will then be asked to grant access.

Documents functions

There are two functions involved in loading the list of files in the UI. The FILE_docs_load Docs function has two tasks: update the workflow with the selected folder so it loads next time and call on FILES.docs.loadFiles, which will return a Flex Table loaded with files.

FILES.docs.loadFiles has arguments app and the ID of the collection you want to get files from. The ID is used so there are no collection name conflicts in the likely case that an approver has a folder with the same name. Passing app makes it possible to run the function without using UiApp.getActiveApplication. FILE_docs_loadDocs does not take arguments because it is run from a handler.

Create a new file named **Docs**, and add it to the namespace:

```
FILE.docs = {};
```

The first function we will build is FILE_docs_loadDocs. This one is fired by a handler and must exist in the global space so you won't be able to add it to the namespace. While using a namespace can greatly reduce the globals in your script and give you a speed boost, we are mainly using it to help keep track of where things are located in the many files that go into a script. Therefore, we can still stick to the naming scheme with little loss in its effect.

When the list box changes value, the execution begins. Get the value of the list box using e.parameter.docsFolder and call on the DocsList service to get the collection the user selected. The collection's URL and ID will be useful later for providing an open link to the user and ensuring we display the right collection regardless of name changes.

```
function FILE_docs_loadDocs(e) {
  var app = UiApp.createApplication(),
      folder = DocsList.getFolder(e.parameter.docsFolder),
      folderUrl = folder.getUrl(),
      folderId = folder.getId();
```

The workflow can't be passed through the handler, but if you remember back when we did the check for the wfId, a new workflow was created and written to the spreadsheet. This means we just need the ID and it can be recalled here.

 Only elements that have an ID or name, depending on the type of element, will be available in e.parameter. There is no way to get the values using app.getElementById, which is only used to set values.

In order to recall the workflow from the spreadsheet, only one value is required, wfId, however, looking back over the doGet file, we have not added any element with the wfId set as a value in an element. A trick to solve this issue is to create a hidden text box and set its value to the current wfId.

Slip back over to the doGet file and create a hidden text box to hold the wfId, making it accessible in e.parameter. The hidden text box can be added anywhere after the creating wfGrid and the cell in row 10 will be used to keep them out of the way of other UI elements.

 One unique attribute of the hidden text box is that it does not take up any space on the page. This means you can slip them in here and there, and no one is the wiser.

While you are here, create a second hidden for the email value that will be used later on to ID the user:

```
wfGrid.setWidget(10,0, app.createHidden().setValue(wfId)
              .setId('wfId').setName('wfId'));
wfGrid.setWidget(11,0, app.createHidden().setValue(email)
              .setId('email').setName('email'));
```

While on the subject of identifying the user, I would like to point out that Google Script has a Session.getActiveUser() method that will allow you to get the user email address if they are signed in and on the same domain as you. This could help you in two ways: you would not need to pass the email in the URL parameters and you could hide the folder selection if the user is not you. You will need to decide for yourself if you want to use this feature or not. For this chapter, the best solution would reach the widest audience. If the publishing settings are set for anonymous then anyone using any email system will be able to use your workflows.

By adding the hidden boxes, you can now load the workflow from the spreadsheet:

```
var wfRowArray = FILE.ssOps.getWfRowFromSS(e.parameter.wfId),
    jsonText = wfRowArray[2],
    workflow = ReLoadJson(jsonText);
```

When the list box change handler runs there are two possible conditions: a value has never been set or the value needs to be changed. Therefore, the first check is to see if there is a collection set at location workflow.getDocsFolders()[0]; if not, add one and set its values. If there is already a collection there, simply update it.

```
if(workflow.getDocsFolders()[0] == undefined){
  workflow.addDocsFolder().setName(e.parameter.docsFolder)
        .setId(folderId).setUrl(folderUrl);
}else{
  workflow.getDocsFolders()[0].setName(e.parameter.docsFolder)
        .setId(folderId).setUrl(folderUrl);
}
```

The changes have been made to the workflow and now it can be written back to the spreadsheet. We also have the information to run FILE.docs.loadFiles, which will be set into the wfGrid at location (4,1):

```
wfRowArray[2] = JSON.stringify(workflow);
FILE.ssOps.setWftoSS(wfRowArray);

app.getElementById('FILE_doGet_wfGrid').setWidget(4,1, FILE.docs.loadFiles(app,
folderId));

return app;
}
```

The second function for loading documents is called by the FILE_docs_loadDocs function and accessed directly from doGet each time it loads as long as a folder has already been set in the workflow.

This function returns a flexTable where each row is an anchor link using the name of the file and its URL. At the end, a link is added to allow the folder to be opened in the case that more files need to be added.

The DocsList makes this very easy to perform. Start by creating a flexTable, get a folder for the provided ID, and then all the files in that folder.

The files array is iterated and each file loaded into the flexTable as an anchor. The filesTable is returned loaded and ready to insert into a cell in the wfGrid.

```
FILE.docs.loadFiles = function(app, folderId){

  var filesTable = app.createFlexTable(),
      folder = DocsList.getFolderById(folderId),
      files = folder.getFiles();

  for (var i in files){
     filesTable.setWidget(parseInt(i),0, app.createAnchor(files[i].getName(),
files[i].getUrl()));
  }

  filesTable.setWidget(parseInt(files.length)+1,1,
                    app.createAnchor('Open Docs collection...', folder.getUrl()));
  return filesTable;
}
```

That wraps up the documents list. Load the published URL and reload the page. Check that selecting a folder refreshes the display and reloading the page with &wfId=*Work flow_ID* brings back the selection, as shown in Figure 8-5.

Making Steps

Workflow steps are the heart of our workflow and also the most complex to code if you want the user to get the most out of using a workflow. The following list will give you a few things you should consider:

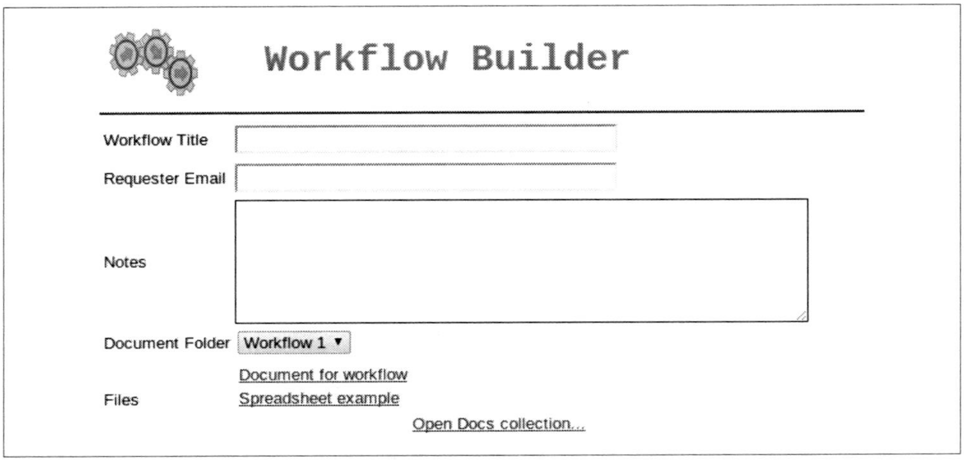

Figure 8-5. The filename links open the document in a new window

- Add steps
- Remove a step
- Insert a step between other steps
- Step details
- Approve a step
- Reject a step
- Step branching
- Dynamically change the direction of the workflow

As you can see, there are many things our workflow will be able to do beyond a simple "Approve" button in an email. This certainly shows off the power of Google Script, but more importantly it gives you an idea of how to write code that allows your applications to dynamically adjust to their environment.

Figure 8-6 shows the different parts of the Steps UI. When the page loads, the script will look for steps in the workflow, run the FILE_steps_loadSteps function, and load a table containing the information about each step. This will also contain a remove link and buttons for approving or rejecting that step. The buttons will only show if the current user's email matches the step. This way you can only perform an operation on a step that is yours. Each step element is built using grids, labels, and buttons and then inserted into a Flex Table, stepsTable, with the other steps much the way each file was added to a table in the Docs section. Finally the stepsTable is placed in cell (6,1) of the wfGrid.

A form, stepForm, will be used to insert steps into the workflow and will be placed in cell (7,1) of the wfGrid. To give the user a cleaner appearance, this form will be hidden on UI load by setting its visibility to false and a button in the next cell below will show

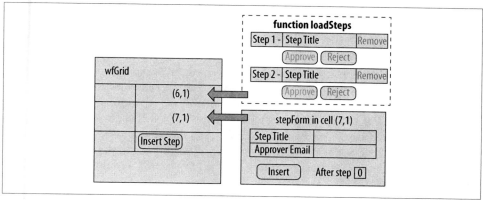

Figure 8-6. The filename links open the document in a new window

the form. This hide and show functionality will be partly run by client side handlers giving it a snappy response.

Steps form

In the doGet file, after loading the documents, we will start creating the form for adding steps. Start by adding a label to give the user a point of reference as to what they are seeing.

```
wfGrid.setWidget(6,0, app.createLabel('Steps'));
```

The stepForm will hold the elements for creating a step. Remember that this form should be hidden when the UI loads so set its visibility to false and add it to the wfGrid.

Create labels and text boxes for the step title and approver email as you would with any form; make sure that the Name and ID are set for each text box.

 The text box for email addresses will take more than one approver in case you need to do branching. The format is **user1@example.com,user2@domain.com**. You will need to train your users on the proper format, or try out the skills you have learned to pick approvers from a list.

The default width of the text box is too short for entering email addresses so stretch them out to 300px. More step details can be added here if you so choose but these are the basics required to make a usable workflow:

```
var stepForm = app.createFlexTable().setVisible(false);
wfGrid.setWidget(7,1, stepForm);

stepForm.setWidget(0, 0, app.createLabel('Step Title'));
stepForm.setWidget(0, 1, app.createTextBox()
                    .setName('FILE_doGet_stepTitle').setId('FILE_doGet_stepTitle').se
```

```
tWidth('300px'));
  stepForm.setWidget(1, 0, app.createLabel('Approver Email'));
  stepForm.setWidget(1, 1, app.createTextBox()
                    .setName('FILE_doGet_approverEmail').setId('FILE_doGet_approverEm
ail').setWidth('300px'));
```

Next we will add an Insert button to the form. To reduce the number of buttons on the UI, a single Insert button will be used in place of having two buttons: one for "Add" and a second for "Insert a step at a certain location." Both operations are the same, but "Add" typically means to append the step at the end. We will use a text box that auto fills with an index location at the end, giving a default behavior of "Add". If the user wants to change that behavior, they can simply change the number in the text box giving an Insert action. For the script, both are the same action and that is why we need only one button.

A (1,3) grid will be used to line up the button, label, and step index text box on a single line (See Figure 8-6). Place the insertGrid in cell (2,1) of the stepForm:

```
  var insertGrid = app.createGrid(1,3).setId('insertGrid');
  stepForm.setWidget(2,1, insertGrid);

  var insertStepButton = app.createButton('Insert')
      .setId('i')
      .addClickHandler(app.createServerClickHandler('FILE_steps_loadSteps')
                    .addCallbackElement(mainGrid));

  insertGrid.setWidget(0,0, insertStepButton);
  insertGrid.setWidget(0,1, app.createLabel(' Insert after step '));
  insertGrid.setWidget(0,2, app.createTextBox()
                    .setName('FILE_doGet_stepIndex').setId('FILE_doGet_stepIndex').se
tWidth('20px'));
```

Take special note of the ID for the button; it is a single i. The FILE_steps_loadSteps function is what you might call a constructor function in Java but here, it will handle all the step related buttons and loading the steps in the UI. More on this later when we create that file, for now, i means Insert.

The handler is a plain old click handler that fires FILE_steps_loadSteps and has main Grid as the callback. Add each element going across the insertGrid using the second number in the arguments to complete the insert step form.

The insert form is hidden from the user; we will use a button to show it. This process uses client side handlers reducing the code, response time, and extra functions normally required by a button. When clicked, the button will need to show the stepForm and hide itself. We use the forTargets method to get the elements already on the UI and forEventSource to get the button.

Client side handlers reduce code, but they are also limited meaning; they can only influence elements already on the UI and use a much smaller set of methods. One huge advantage is the ability to stack elements in the `forTargets` argument (for example, `forTargets(button1, button2, grid)`). Another advantage to client handlers is that they work right along side the server handlers.

The `showInsertForm` button is added to the `wfGrid` in the cell below the step form so that clicking it causes the form to appear under the mouse.

```
var showInsertForm = app.createButton('Insert Step')
    .addClickHandler(app.createClientHandler()
                    .forTargets(stepForm)
                    .setVisible(true))
    .addClickHandler(app.createClientHandler()
                    .forEventSource().setVisible(false));
wfGrid.setWidget(8,1, showInsertForm);
```

After filling out the insert step form and clicking the button, the form should be hidden and the button that opens the form shown, a reset so to speak. This could be done in the `FILE_steps_loadSteps` function when it returns, but it is much more efficient to take care of this on the client side. Add click handlers to the `insertStepButton` that utilize the client handlers to toggle the visibility.

```
insertStepButton.addClickHandler(app.createClientHandler()
                .forTargets(stepForm).setVisible(false))
        .addClickHandler(app.createClientHandler()
                .forTargets(showInsertForm).setVisible(true));
```

The insert step form parts are in place and you can now reload the published page and try out the show/hide function. When you click the Insert button on the form shown in Figure 8-7, you will get an error from the server telling you that there is no `FILE_steps_loadSteps` function to run. We will take care of that next. For now, simply dismiss the error.

Document Folder	Workflow 1 ▼	
Files	Document for workflow	
	Spreadsheet example	
	Open Docs collection...	
Steps		
	Step Title	
	Approver Email	
	Insert Insert after step	

Figure 8-7. The complete step form

Loading the steps

The form built in the last section will need a function to process inserting a record and the steps need to be loaded into the UI. In this section, you will learn how to do process button presses from the form and those created dynamically for each of the steps. Using a single function will greatly reduce the amount of code required and help to keep things organized.

Create a new file, name it **Steps**, set its namespace, and click Run to grant access.

```
FILE.steps = {};
```

The Steps file will be laid out in two larger sections of code as shown in Figure 8-8. This will help you as we work through the nearly 200 lines of upcoming code. I know it might seem like a lot, but it has a modular feel that gives you the structure to understand it clearly.

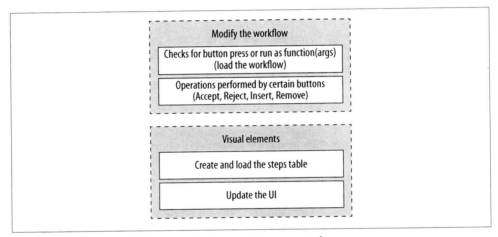

Figure 8-8. The filename links open the document in a new window

When a handler runs a function, it passes one argument, which is typically called e as seen in FILE_steps_loadSteps(e). The argument will have all the named elements contained in e.parameter giving us a way to read the values of the various elements. However, this takes pressing a button or other user action to accomplish. If you want to run a function during the loading of the UI, then you will need to pass the elements you need through the arguments as in FILE_steps_loadSteps(e, wfId, app).

The problem comes in when deciding what UiApp you need to use. For handlers, like a button press, you must get the active UI, app = UiApp.getActiveApplication(). On the other hand, running the function without a handler you must pass the UI though the function's arguments. To figure out which type of event, handled or direct, you must use at least two arguments in the direct method. The second one does not need to actually pass anything as long as it has a value (for example, directFunction(app, 'true')). This way the second argument can be evaluated for undefined. In the case of a handler, there is not a second argument so it always returns undefined telling us that it was a handler.

Inspect the `if` statement in the first few lines of code. `if(wfId == undefined)`, the second argument, `wfId` can only have a value if the function is called directly. Therefore an undefined value means we should treat it as being sent from a handler and load the active UI. We will also need to get values from `e` as seen when getting the workflow ID, `e.parameter.wfId`.

```
function FILE_step_loadSteps(e, wfId, app){

  if(wfId == undefined){
    var app = UiApp.getActiveApplication(),
        wfId = e.parameter.wfId;
  }
```

We don't need an else statement here because if `wfId` is defined, the values are already provided in the arguments.

Knowing where to get the workflow ID, we can now load the correct workflow from the spreadsheet and make it into an object.

```
var wfRowArray = FILE.ssOps.getWfRowFromSS(wfId),
    jsonText = wfRowArray[2],
    workflow = ReLoadJson(jsonText);
```

Now that the workflow is loaded and ready, we can start performing operations on it. Our workflow would not be much without steps so a good place to start the next section is by inserting a step.

In our application, only a button presses cause a change to the workflow so we can cut out any function runs by checking to see if `e.parameter` is present.

```
if(e.parameter != undefined){

  //Insert start notification code here
```

You will see a few notification comments left in the code while working through this section. The notifications will be bolted on later and these markers will help you see where they go.

Each button that executes `FILE_steps_loadSteps` will start with a unique letter we set when giving the button its ID. For example, the ID for the insert button is `i`. We will use a series of `if` statements and regular expressions to figure out which button was pressed. When the function runs `/^i/i.test(e.parameter.source)` will return true if the button's ID started with "i".

To insert a step, call on the Workflow Class `insertStep` method, which takes the step index as an argument. Because this call returns the newly created step, the variable `step` can now be used to add more attributes.

The approvers text box takes email addresses separated by commas, which will need to be split into an array that is used to add the approvers for this step. Set their status to Pending, same as the status for the step.

The workflow object now contains the new step, but that only exists in RAM so to speak, so you need to save it back to the spreadsheet as a JSON string.

```
//insert step
    if(/^i/i.test(e.parameter.source)){
      step = workflow.insertStep(e.parameter.FILE_doGet_stepIndex)
                    .setTitle(e.parameter.FILE_doGet_stepTitle)
                    .setStatus('Pending');
      var approvers = e.parameter.FILE_doGet_approverEmail.split(',');
      for(g in approvers){
        step.addApprover().setEmail(approvers[g])
                    .setApprovalStatus('Pending');
      }
      //Save WF
      wfRowArray[2] = JSON.stringify(workflow);
      FILE.ssOps.setWftoSS(wfRowArray);
    }

    //add more button methods here


  }
  //add the UI load feature here

  return app;
}
```

By closing a few of the brackets, we can give this a test run and see that the steps are being created in the spreadsheet. Please note that as we continue through this section, code will be added where the comments are instead of at the end.

Reload the published URL with a `wfId` appended and create a step as shown in Figure 8-9.

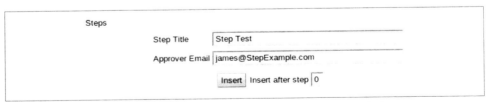

Figure 8-9. Here the step form is filled with information and will be inserted after step zero

Make sure to set the index to "0" and click Insert. Nothing will change on the UI, but if you go to the spreadsheet holding the workflow data you will see that a new step has been added in the steps array section similar to this example: `"steps":[{"approvers":` `[{"email":"james@StepExample.com","approvalStatus":"Pending"}],` `"title":"Step` `Test","status":"Pending"}]`.

He giveth and he taketh away; the remove function will be the next button to process. The remove feature will get a d for delete. We won't be creating the remove link until later, but for now know that its ID will start with a "d". Notice I said "start with," to figure out which step to remove the link IDs will be created dynamically using their index numbers. Therefore the first workflow step removal link will have an ID of d0. More on this when we create the links.

To separate off the d, use `e.parameter.source.substring(1)`.

This should tell you that while our code can only figure out 26 different types of button presses, the number of remove, approve, and reject buttons are endless.

```
//remove step
    else if(/^d/i.test(e.parameter.source)){
      workflow.removeStep(e.parameter.source.substring(1));
      //Save WF
      wfRowArray[2] = JSON.stringify(workflow);
      FILE.ssOps.setWftoSS(wfRowArray);
    }
```

Once the step is removed by its index number, the workflow is saved.

The next two functions will deal with the approval and rejection buttons. They are a bit more complicated because the approver must be identified in order to get the process going in the right direction.

Starting with the approval function, `e.parameter.source` is tested for beginning with a and then the step index number is taken as the substring. This means you know the step that has come in for approval and the notification system we build later in the chapter will have added the approver's email to the URL where we can get it using `e.parameter.email`. One thing we will need to know is if all the approvers have given their OK and that this is the one that completes the step. Remember a step can have many approvers separated by commas when creating the step. Two things you know are the number of approvers in the approver array and their status. What is needed now is a counter to check these two values. Create a variable **var stepComplete = 0;**, which will be incremented as the approvers are processed.

We get the correct step from the workflow by the index number and iterate the approvers until one is found matching the approver email. Once found, the approver is marked with the "Approved" status. As each approver is being checked against the email we can also look to see if they have approved and increment the counter.

Once the approvers are done being checked, an `if` statement compares the stepComplete counter to the number of steps. A match means this step is complete and can be marked as so.

Because the status of the approvers and steps are changing this also means the overall status of the workflow can change. A similar counter to the one used for approvers is implemented to find and mark the workflow complete if all the steps have made final approval.

The finishing up of the approval function is writing the changes to the spreadsheet and sending a notice. The notice is sent here to trigger the notification system to run and evaluate the changes made to see if more emails should be sent.

```
//approve step
    else if(/^a/i.test(e.parameter.source)){
        var stepNumber = parseInt(e.parameter.source.substring(1));

        var stepComplete = 0;
        for (i in workflow.getSteps()[stepNumber].getApprovers()){
            if (workflow.getSteps()[stepNumber].getApprovers()[i].getEmail() ==
e.parameter.email){
                workflow.getSteps()[stepNumber].getApprovers()
[i].setApprovalStatus('Approved');
            }
            if (workflow.getSteps()[stepNumber].getApprovers()[i].getApprovalStatus() ==
'Approved'){
                stepComplete++
            }
        }
        if(stepComplete == workflow.getSteps()[stepNumber].getApprovers().length){
            workflow.getSteps()[stepNumber].setStatus('Complete');
        }

        var wfComplete = 0
        for (w in workflow.getSteps()){
            if(workflow.getSteps()[w].getStatus() == 'Complete')
                wfComplete++
        }
        if (wfComplete == workflow.getSteps().length){
            workflow.setStatus('Complete');
            wfRowArray[1] = 'Complete';
        }

        //Save workFlow
        wfRowArray[2] = JSON.stringify(workflow);
        FILE.ssOps.setWftoSS(wfRowArray);

        //Save for sending notice

    }
```

Once you start your workflow, I'm sure you would like nothing more than to have it go along peacefully through each step until it has completed. The reality is that a workflow should have the ability to go back and forth or even to other people if necessary, and to make it go back, we use the rejection button.

Don't tell the boss but it is less work, for the script anyhow, to go backward than it is to go forward. This is because you will simply set the values of the previous step back to "Pending."

Start off the same as in the approval function by getting the source, only this time it is an **r**. See the naming dilemma between remove, (d) for delete, and reject, (r) for reject. I guess the remove link could have said "delete" and you will get to make that choice just ahead when we build the display UI section.

Exactly like setting an approved status, now set status to Rejected. In the next part, get the step minus one `workflow.getSteps()[stepNumber-1]` and set the approval status to "Pending" for all approvers.

Rejection is a tricky business to guess ahead of time because you don't know what the condition might be a week or even a year down the road when that point is reached. To accommodate for changes, the approver can insert a step before or after their step, creating a different direction. If the project is rejected but needs to go to a new employee, the approver inserts a step before their own and clicks Reject. The script will know what to do next.

It is important to set the previous step to rejected so that the notification system knows which email to send to the approver of that step. Again, save a line to give the notification system a kick.

```
//reject step
    else if(/^r/i.test(e.parameter.source)){
       var stepNumber = parseInt(e.parameter.source.substring(1));

       for (i in workflow.getSteps()[stepNumber].getApprovers()){
          if (workflow.getSteps()[stepNumber].getApprovers()[i].getEmail() ==
e.parameter.email){
             workflow.getSteps()[stepNumber].getApprovers()
[i].setApprovalStatus('Rejected');
          }
       }
       for (i in workflow.getSteps()[stepNumber-1].getApprovers()){
          workflow.getSteps()[stepNumber-1].getApprovers()
[i].setApprovalStatus('Pending');
       }
       workflow.getSteps()[stepNumber-1].setStatus('Rejected');

       //Save WF
       wfRowArray[2] = JSON.stringify(workflow);
       FILE.ssOps.setWftoSS(wfRowArray);

       //Save for sending notice

    }
 }
```

That is all the functions we have for this application, but you should be getting an idea about how to add more button presses and read their source. For example, a poke button could be added if you think the workflow is bogged down and needs some encouragement.

With operations out of the way, we need to do some visual stuff like creating the buttons you just finished writing functions for. This section builds a display much like what was used in Docs, but with more logic to determine which buttons show given the user viewing the page.

Each step has many elements to display and that means several grids and tables will need to be set inside each other to create the UI, as shown in Figure 8-10.

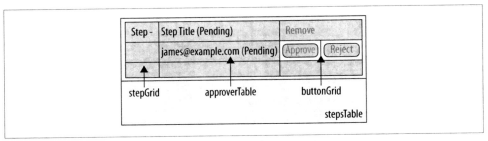

Figure 8-10. Nesting grids works much like using tables in HTML

All of the steps will be held in the Flex Table `stepsTable`, one step for each row. This table will be added to the `wfGrid` that was created on load of the `doGet` function. To fill the `stepsTable` we use a `for` loop and iterate the workflow steps. The next nested grid will hold the details and buttons associated to a certain step.

```
var stepsTable = app.createFlexTable().setId('stepsTable');

for (i in workflow.getSteps()){
  var stepGrid = app.createGrid(3,4);
  stepsTable.setWidget(parseInt(i),0,stepGrid);
```

The containers are ready and can be filled with step information. Steps are an array with parameters added to them; they are zero-based like any other JavaScript array, so to display a step number on the UI we use `parseInt(i)+1` where `i` is the number of the step. Add a few labels to describe the step and its status in the first row "0" of the `stepGrid`.

```
stepGrid.setWidget(0,0, app.createLabel('Step '+ (parseInt(i)+1)+' - '));
stepGrid.setWidget(0,1, app.createLabel(
                 workflow.getSteps()[i].getTitle() +' '+
                 ' ('+workflow.getSteps()[i].getStatus()+') '
                 ));
```

Remember those button functions you created? Now you finally get to make the actual buttons to execute them. Well, two buttons and a link to give the UI some style. The first one we add is the remove link. The buttons will execute the `FILE_steps_load`

`Steps` function. Look closely at the `setId` argument, which uses a letter plus the step iteration number. That is how we know which button was pressed on a given step. Surprisingly simple, and should be clear to you now that you can see the whole picture. All of the buttons will affect the `stepsTable` so we load that as the callback.

```
stepGrid.setWidget(0,2, app.createLabel('remove step').setId('d'+i)
                    .setStyleAttribute('color', 'red')
                    .addClickHandler(app.createServerClickHandler('FILE_steps_l
   oadSteps')
                    .addCallbackElement(stepsTable)));
```

The approver and their status are also important information especially if there are several approvers in a certain step. When things aren't moving along we know just who to point the finger at.

There may be several approvers and the best way to display them is by going down the page. Again we only have one cell in the `stepGrid` for this information so yet another Flex Table will be inserted.

Get the approvers in step `i` and iterate them adding each to the `approverTable`.

```
var approverTable = app.createFlexTable();
stepGrid.setWidget(1,1, approverTable);

for(s in workflow.getSteps()[i].getApprovers()){
  approverTable.setWidget(parseInt(s),0, app.createLabel(workflow
              .getSteps()[i].getApprovers()[s].getEmail()+' ('+
              workflow.getSteps()[i].getApprovers()[s].getApprovalStatus()
  +') ')));
```

The approve and reject buttons should go next to each other, which will require a (1,2) grid. Add the buttons and place the `buttonGrid` at cell (i,1) of the `approverTable`:

```
var buttonGrid = app.createGrid(1,2);
approverTable.setWidget(parseInt(s),1, buttonGrid);
```

We need a little logic to help sort out which buttons will be shown depending on the user. This is because we don't want them approving the wrong workflow.

What we need is a simple state engine that will look at the different possibilities and not load the buttons if they are not needed. The user should only see an approval button if they are the approver for that step. This keeps them from making a rejection after approving a step and messing up the sequence. It also makes it clear which step is the one requiring their attention. Once they make a choice, the button should disappear. No do-overs here because we are sending emails to the next parties right after the button press. We also don't want to reject step 0 because there is no one for it to go back to. This takes care of the approver level.

The next part of our state engine will look at the step level to ensure that buttons are not shown if the previous step is pending or rejected. This way, if the approver has two roles where they may get the workflow back at some later step, we don't want them to see those later buttons until that step is ready.

```
if (e.parameter != undefined){
  if(workflow.getSteps()[i].getApprovers()[s].getEmail() == e.parameter.email &&
     workflow.getSteps()[parseInt(i)].getStatus() != 'Complete'){

    var showApprove = true;
    if(i != 0){
      if(workflow.getSteps()[parseInt(i)-1].getStatus() == 'Pending' ||
         workflow.getSteps()[parseInt(i)-1].getStatus() == 'Rejected'){
        showApprove = false;
      }
    }

    if(showApprove){
        buttonGrid.setWidget(0,0, app.createButton('Approve').setId('a'+i)
                      .setStyleAttribute('color', 'green')
                      .addClickHandler(app.createServerClickHandler('FILE_ste
ps_loadSteps')
                      .addCallbackElement(stepsTable)));
    }

    if (i != 0 && showApprove){
        buttonGrid.setWidget(0,1, app.createButton('Reject').setId('r'+i)
                      .setStyleAttribute('color', 'red')
                      .addClickHandler(app.createServerClickHandler('FILE_ste
ps_loadSteps')
                      .addCallbackElement(stepsTable)));

      }
    }
  }
}
```

When we entered the steps file we needed to know if it was from a button press UI page load. Similarly the buttons above will not know anything outside the stepsTable passed in the callback. That means we will need to stick a few hidden values in the table for the buttons to know the details for which user and workflow they have.

```
stepsTable.setWidget(parseInt(workflow.getSteps().length)+1,0,
app.createHidden().setValue(wfId)
                .setId('wfId').setName('wfId'));
if (e.parameter != undefined){
  stepsTable.setWidget(parseInt(workflow.getSteps().length)+2,0,
app.createHidden().setValue(e.parameter.email)
                .setId('email').setName('email'));
}
```

If you glanced at the end of the next code block you are likely excited to have spied the end of this function. Almost 200 lines of code in one function can be intimidating but you have pulled through.

This last part is simply writing the stepsTable back to the wfTable and setting the text boxes in the step form to empty strings so the user will not need to delete the last values. As a matter of UI goodness we will set the insert after index to the number of steps in the workflow. This way the user can change the step insert point, but the default will always be to add after the last step.

```
app.getElementById('FILE_doGet_wfGrid').setWidget(6,1, stepsTable);
app.getElementById('FILE_doGet_stepTitle').setValue('');
app.getElementById('FILE_doGet_approverEmail').setValue('');

app.getElementById('FILE_doGet_stepIndex').setValue((workflow.getSteps().length).toSt
ring());

    return app;
}
```

You are almost there!

To get the Steps UI to load we need to add a line back over in the doGet file. Down at the end, just before returning the app, you need to run the FILE_steps_loadSteps function to get any steps that are already saved.

```
FILE_steps_loadSteps(e, wfId, app);
```

That has been a lot of hard work and now it is time to test it out. This will be a bit of a mock up but it is the best way to make sure all the parts are working correctly.

Reload the published page while ensuring &wfId=*yourId* is on the end of the URL in the address bar. Click the Insert Step button and enter several steps with approver emails, as shown in Figure 8-11.

 You can NOT have the same approver in consecutive steps; that should make sense but sometimes in testing we don't think about why that condition can't exist.

Because the workflow handles branching (multiple approvers) it would be a good idea to test out that function.

	Step 1 - Starting out (Pending)	remove step
	test1@example.com (Pending)	
	Step 2 - Halfway point (Pending)	remove step
	test2@example.com (Pending)	
Steps	Step 3 - Final Approval (Pending)	remove step
	test1@example.com (Pending)	
	test3@example.com (Pending)	

Figure 8-11. You will not see the approve and reject buttons because no email has been given in the URL parameters.

Each time you add a step, the UI gets an update. Try removing a step and inserting another in its place.

Once you are satisfied with the steps it is time to test out the state engine. At the end of the URL add **&email=*test1@example.com*** or whatever email address you used for Step 1 and reload the page. The state engine will now display the Approve button for the first step. Remember there is no Reject button for step 1.

Click the Approve button. The button vanishes and the Approved status is shown by the approver's email address. If this was the only approver for that step then you will see that the step is also marked complete.

Change the email in the URL to an approver in the second step and continue testing. Perhaps try a rejection, as shown in Figure 8-12, where test3@example.com has rejected the step returning it to test2@example.com.

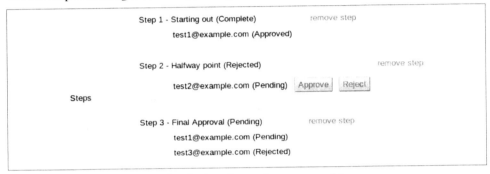

Figure 8-12. Rejecting a step sends it back to the previous approver(s)

Saving the Workflow

There is something missing. While the documents and steps are saved in the spreadsheet, we have not created a Save button for the workflow information. This section will cover the final save and updating the information so that notes can be added to the workflow at anytime.

At the end of the doGet file before `return app;`, create a button and add it to the wfGrid. This button will execute `FILE_saveWorkflow_save`:

```
var saveButton = app.createButton('Save Workflow')
    .setId('saveButton')
    .addClickHandler(app.createServerClickHandler('FILE_saveWorkflow_save')
                .addCallbackElement(wfGrid));
wfGrid.setWidget(9,0, saveButton);
```

Create a new file, name it **Save Workflow**, and click Run to authorize it. You can now set up the namespace and the function `FILE_saveWorkflow_save`. Like many of the other functions in this script, this one starts with getting the workflow from the spreadsheet.

Now we can start setting the values from the UI into the workflow:

```
FILE.saveWorkflow = {};
```

```
function FILE_saveWorkflow_save(e) {
  var app = UiApp.getActiveApplication(),
      wfRowArray = FILE.ssOps.getWfRowFromSS(e.parameter.wfId),
      jsonText = wfRowArray[2],
      workflow = ReLoadJson(jsonText);

  workflow.setTitle(e.parameter.wfTitle)
          .setStatus('Pending')
          .setRequester(e.parameter.wfRequester)
          .setNote(e.parameter.wfNote);
```

We set the status in the workflow object to Pending, but that has not been written to the spreadsheet yet, giving us an opportunity to check and see if this is a first time save of the workflow.

```
if(wfRowArray[1]== 'New'){
```

If the workflow is new, then we are going to send an email to the requester letting them know that they created a workflow and how to get to it. We also want to give them a page with similar details and a link to load the workflow in case they want to keep editing. This is done so that the wfId gets into the URL. We don't start the workflow yet, that gets its own link in case the requester wants to wait before pulling the trigger.

To start the workflow we will need a start trigger in the URL sent in the email and on the UI:

```
var startLink = FILE.settings.publishedUrl+'&wfId='+e.parameter.wfId
+'&start=true';
```

Go back to the Steps file and look around line 20 for the comment and add the start code to kick the notify function into action. After we get these emails sent we begin the notification system, so please hang in there.

```
//Insert start notification code here
if(e.parameter.start == 'true'){
  workflow = FILE.notifications.notify(wfId);
}
```

Continuing in the Save Workflow file, it is time to create an HTML email message.

 If you really want to dress up the email notifications you can write your template in HTML and import it as a string. Using key values, special strings (for example, %email%) you can run the JavaScript replace method to add your workflow values to the template.

Our email template will be simple enough, so hardcoding it is a great option.

```
var html =
            '<body>'+
              '<h2>You just created a workflow.</h2><br />' +
              '<b>Workflow title:</b> '+ workflow.getTitle()+'<br />' +
              '<b>Notes:</b> '+ workflow.getNote()+'<br />' +
              '<br />';
```

```
var folder = DocsList.getFolderById(workflow.getDocsFolders()[0].getId());
var files = folder.getFiles();

if(files.length >= 1){
    html += '<b>Documents:</b><br />'
    for(k in files){
        html += '  <a href="'+files[k].getUrl()+'">'+
                            files[k].getName()+'</a><br />';
    }
}
html +=
    '<a href="'+folder.getUrl()+'">Open folder...</a><br />'+
    '<br />'+
    '<b>Steps:</b><br />';

for(j in workflow.getSteps()){
    html += '  Step '+(parseInt(j)+1)+ ' - '+workflow.getSteps()
[j].getTitle()+'<br />';
    }

html +=
    '<br />'+
    'Visit the link below to START, view the progress or edit your workflow<br /
>'+
        '<h2><a href="'+startLink+'">Start Workflow</a></h2>' +
        '<br />'+
        '<br />'+
    '<a href="'+FILE.settings.publishedUrl+'">Create more Workflows</a><br />'+
        '<a href="'+FILE.settings.publishedUrl+'&wfId='+e.parameter.wfId+'">Edit
this Workflow</a>'+
        '</body>';
```

If you don't know any HTML that may look a bit scary, but it is basically formatting and using the variables from the workflow to create links.

Sending the email is one line of code using the MailApp:

```
MailApp.sendEmail(e.parameter.wfRequester, 'Workflow Created', '', {htmlBody:
html});
```

 When adding services like MailApp you need to run the script from the Editor to grant access to the service or you will get authorization errors in the UI. See Figure 8-13.

The email is off and we need to display the information on the screen as well. This will be done using a Flex Table that replaces the current UI.

```
var savedTable = app.createFlexTable();
var saveText = app.createLabel('Workflow Saved');
savedTable.setWidget(0, 0, saveText);
FILE.css.setStyle(saveText, FILE.css.submitTy);
savedTable.setWidget(1,0, app.createAnchor('Click here to START the workflow',
startLink));
```

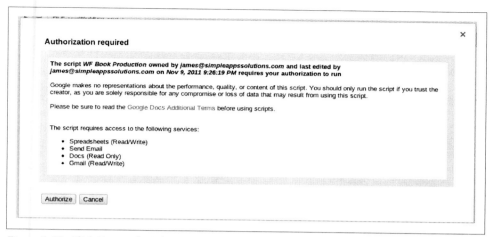

Figure 8-13. Click Run in the Editor any time you get an authentication warning in the UI

```
        savedTable.setWidget(2, 0, app.createLabel('You have been sent an email if you
would like to start the workflow later'));
        savedTable.setWidget(3,0, app.createAnchor('EDIT the workflow',
FILE.settings.publishedUrl+'&wfId='+e.parameter.wfId));

        app.getElementById(FILE_doGet_mainGrid).setWidget(1,0, savedTable);
    }
```

Basic stuff here, add a few labels to tell the user what just happened and make anchors they can click to get the process rolling. The savedTable is then set to the content section of the mainGrid.

To wrap things up we just need a quick write to the spreadsheet:

```
    wfRowArray[1] = 'Pending';
    wfRowArray[2] = JSON.stringify(workflow);
    FILE.ssOps.setWftoSS(wfRowArray);

    return app;
}
```

Take note of the if brackets surrounding the email and UI update. If this is not a first time save and the user has returned to add a comment in the notes, clicking Save will only save the changes and not send emails.

Figure 8-14 shows the completed UI ready to save the workflow.

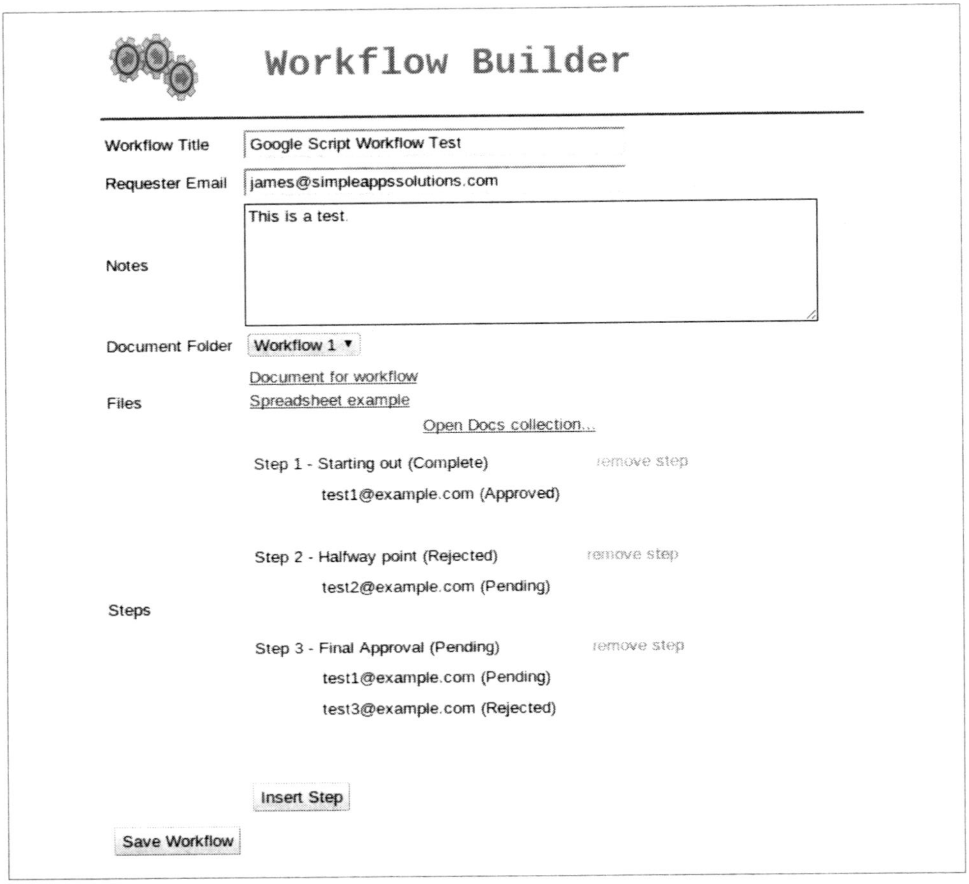

Workflow Builder

Workflow Title	Google Script Workflow Test
Requester Email	james@simpleappssolutions.com
Notes	This is a test.
Document Folder	Workflow 1 ▼
Files	Document for workflow Spreadsheet example Open Docs collection...

Steps	Step 1 - Starting out (Complete) remove step
	        test1@example.com (Approved)
	
	Step 2 - Halfway point (Rejected) remove step
	        test2@example.com (Pending)
	
	Step 3 - Final Approval (Pending) remove step
	        test1@example.com (Pending)
	        test3@example.com (Rejected)

Insert Step

Save Workflow

Figure 8-14. Time to hit the Save button

After clicking Save, you will see a new screen, Figure 8-15, with the instructions for starting the workflow.

Workflow Builder

Workflow Saved
Click here to START the workflow
You have been sent an email if you would like to start the workflow later
EDIT the workflow

Figure 8-15. The "Workflow Saved" page gives the user an opportunity to start a new workflow or edit the current one

If your plan is to start the workflow at a later time, then an email has also been sent with details about the workflow and the link to get started. See Figure 8-16.

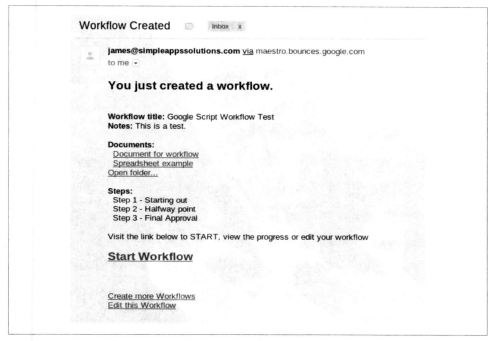

Figure 8-16. An email is a great way for users to understand what has been created in the UI

The HTML looks great when you see it without the tags. The UI is now complete and working; all we need now is a notification system to send emails depending on the status of the workflow.

Notification System

The workflow is fully operational but it only sends an email to the person who created it. This section will go into the details of sending notifications depending on the status of the workflow.

Before we jump in, go back to the Steps file and dig out those notification comments. They will be in the approve and reject functions, around lines 80 and 100. Insert the notify call:

```
//Send Notice
workflow = FILE.notifications.notify(wfId);
```

Open a new file, name it **Notifications**, and set its namespace.

For greater flexibility we use an `if` statement to determine how the `wfId` is being sent into the function and load it into its own variable. That will allow us to load the current workflow. You never know when this workflow will get reloaded and if it has been completed, we don't want it sending out any more emails. If the workflow status reaches the Complete stage, it simply gets returned.

```
FILE.notifications = {};

FILE.notifications.notify = function(e) {

  if(e.parameter == undefined){
    var wfId = e;
  }else{
    var wfId = e.parameter.wfId;
  }

  //Load the workflow
  var wfRowArray = FILE.ssOps.getWfRowFromSS(wfId),
      jsonText = wfRowArray[2],
      workflow = ReLoadJson(jsonText);

  //workflow is complete
  if(workflow.getStatus() == 'Complete')
    return workflow;
```

The whole intent of this notification system is to send emails, but it will need to perform a status check on the workflow to make sure the right emails go out. If you remember the Steps file handles user decisions. Therefore, we will make a series of checks.

Start by iterating the steps in the workflow. There are two types of steps we should send emails for, an approval request and if the step has been rejected. For the user this information will come through in the subject line of the email.

```
var steps = workflow.getSteps();
for(i in steps){

  if(steps[i].getStatus() == 'Pending'){
    var subject = 'Workflow approval required for ' + workflow.getTitle();
  }else if(steps[i].getStatus() == 'Rejected'){
    var subject = 'The workflow ' + workflow.getTitle() + ' has been rejected';
  }
```

Subject line in place, we can now determine who gets the email. Certainly not a complete step, so we iterate over those until coming to a step that has a value other than Complete. In truth, they can only be Pending, Rejected, and Complete.

Each approver also has a status and we want to only send emails to those who are Pending and Rejected.

```
if(steps[i].getStatus() != 'Complete'){
  var approvers = steps[i].getApprovers()
  for(j in approvers){
```

```
if(approvers[j].getApprovalStatus() == 'Pending' ||
    approvers[j].getApprovalStatus() == 'Rejected'){
```

Similar to the HTML email that was sent in the save function, we will be sending approvers an email encoded with information about the workflow and a link to manage their choices. Note that because we have gotten the workflow, we can pull out the folder ID for docs and put those files right in the email as links.

```
var link = FILE.settings.publishedUrl +'&wfId='+wfId+'&email='+
    approvers[j].getEmail();

var html =
    '<body>'+
        '<h2>You have been asked to approve a workflow.</h2><br />' +
        '<b>Workflow title:</b> '+ workflow.getTitle()+'<br />' +
        '<b>Requester:</b> '+ workflow.getRequester()+'<br />' +
        '<b>Step name:</b> '+ steps[i].getTitle()+' ('+(parseInt(i)+1)+'/'+
            steps.length+')<br />' +
        '<b>Notes:</b> '+ workflow.getNote()+'<br />' +
        '<br />';

var folder = DocsList.getFolderById(workflow.getDocsFolders()[0].getId());
var files = folder.getFiles();

if(files.length >= 1){
    html += '<b>Documents:</b><br />'
    for(k in files){
        html += '  <a href="'+files[k].getUrl()+'">'+
                        files[k].getName()+'</a><br />';
    }
}
html +=
    '<a href="'+folder.getUrl()+'">Open folder...</a><br /><br />'+
    '<h2><a href="'+link+'">Click to Open Workflow</a></h2>' +
    '</body>';
```

The mail app will come to the rescue again and happily send our message. To understand who has been sent an email, we will set the approvers status to "Email sent."

```
MailApp.sendEmail(approvers[j].getEmail(), subject, '', {htmlBody:
html});
    workflow.getSteps()[i].getApprovers()[j].setApprovalStatus('Email
Sent');
    }
}
```

Having found a step that has pending approvers, we don't want to go past here so the loop is broken. We changed the status of the approvers that got emails and so the workflow needs to be saved. It is also important that we return the modified workflow in the call to avoid doing a second get workflow.

```
    break;
    }
}
//Save workflow
```

```
    wfRowArray[2] = JSON.stringify(workflow);
    FILE.ssOps.setWftoSS(wfRowArray);
    return workflow;
}
```

We have run out of code, so let's get to testing!

Load up the published URL with no parameters. This tells the application that we are creating a new workflow. Fill out the form and add a few steps. Make sure to use emails that work and that you can check on. Click Save and then the "Start workflow" link. We are on our way.

The UI should load in a new window and the first approver will have the status "Email Sent." Figure 8-17 shows the email sent after starting the workflow.

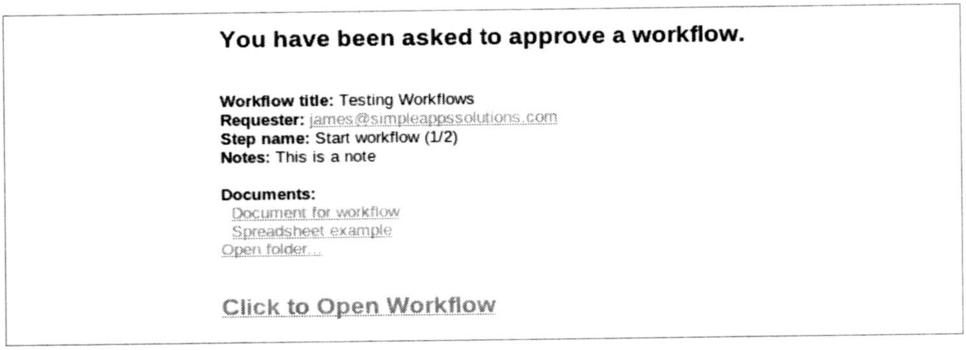

You have been asked to approve a workflow.

Workflow title: Testing Workflows
Requester: james@simpleappssolutions.com
Step name: Start workflow (1/2)
Notes: This is a note

Documents:
 Document for workflow
 Spreadsheet example
Open folder...

Click to Open Workflow

Figure 8-17. It works!

CHAPTER 9

Mash Up

Directing Email Using Google Forms

Google Forms are a very convenient way to quickly get information into a spreadsheet. Add some Google Script and you can turbo charge that form to send email notifications, generate other data in the spreadsheet, and all those things you might want to do when getting data from a form.

In this section you will learn the basics of getting form information into a Google Script and sending an email depending on a selection from a drop down list in the Google form.

Highlights:

- Google Forms
- EmailApp
- Event Triggers

Open up a Google spreadsheet and start creating a form. The example we will use is for routing inquiries to the right department: Sales or Service. Figure 9-1 shows the form editor and the drop down box selection.

After creating the form you can return to the spreadsheet to see the form fields have become columns in the spreadsheet. See Figure 9-2.

Now open the Script Editor (Tools→Script editor).

You can delete the default function and start the script with global variables (outside any function) that will contain the email addresses for the correct department.

```
var sales = 'sales@example.com';
var service = 'service@example.com';
//add more as needed
```

Now create a notify function that will be used to send the emails. Don't forget the e parameter, which will be used later in this section to pass form submit values.

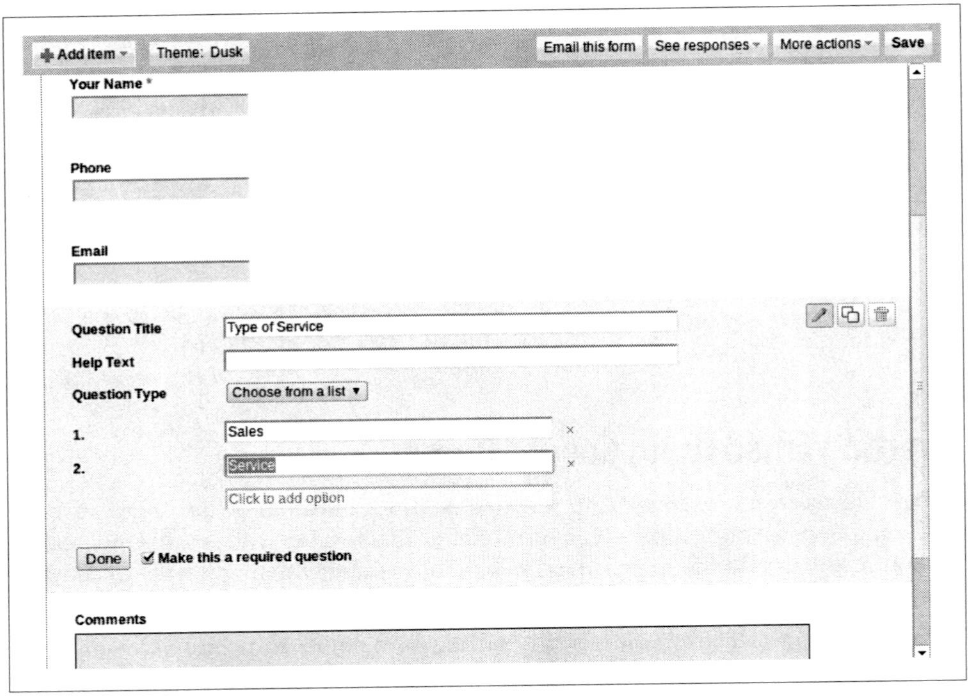

Figure 9-1. Google forms can be inserted into most websites and emailed

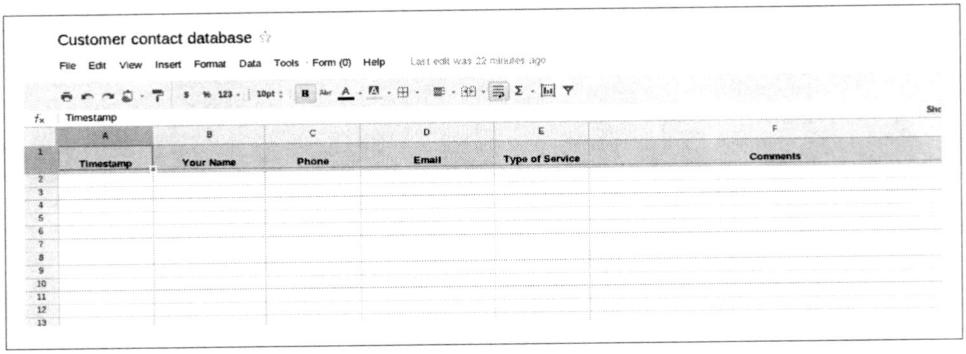

Figure 9-2. Note the timestamp is automatically added

Create a variable to hold the selected department. Next, add a JavaScript switch, which is much more efficient in this case than stacking `if` statements.

The switch argument is where we need to get the value from the form when it is submitted. These values are passed in the parameter `e.values`, which is a zero-based array that looks like this: `["2011/11/17 13:00", "James", "555-5555", "cus tomer@gmail.com", "Sales", "comments"]`. As you may have guessed, the spreadsheet columns line up with these values in a zero-based array.

If you get confused over which number in the array lines up with a certain form field, just count from the top on the form. The timestamp, which is not on the form, is always in `e.values[0]`.

Looking at the form, location 4 is the list box containing the department. Use this in the switch arguments. In a switch, you use cases with the value you hope to match. Yes, they are case sensitive if you were thinking to ask. All that needs to be done for this simple script is to set the value of email to the correct department variable from above. Don't forget to `break;` at the end of each case or you will run the next case as well.

```
function notify(e) {
  var email = '';

  switch (e.values[4]){

        case 'Sales':
          email = sales;
        break;

        case 'Service':
          email = service;
        break;
  }
```

When sending an email to the correct department it would be great to also add the details of the request so they don't need to go to the spreadsheet. You can use HTML in the body of the messages you send and this helps you to make a nice presentation for your staff.

Simply add your field variables to the correct places in the HTML template. If you would like a more complex template, consider using a template file and key values as described in Chapter 6.

```
var html =
    '<body>'+
    '<h2>Please contact: '+ e.values[1] +'</h2>'+
    'Comment: <br />'+
    e.values[5] + '<br />'+
    '<br />'+
    'Phone: ' + e.values[2] + '<br />'+
    'Email: ' + e.values[3] + '<br />'+
    '</body>';
```

All that is left is to send the email using the MailApp service. To customize the subject, add the type of request using `e.values[4]` in the second argument:

```
MailApp.sendEmail(email, "Information Request: "+e.values[4] , 'No html body );',
{htmlBody: html});
}
```

Save the script and run it once to grant permission for MailApp. Now that the form and script are ready, it is time to set up a form submit trigger. In the menu, click Triggers➞Current script triggers, and in the pop-up window, select "Click here to add one now."

Figure 9-3 shows the triggers dialog box where you will need to select the notify function and on form submit from the list boxes. Click Save.

Figure 9-3. You can also set time-based triggers here

Once again you have added tremendous functionality to your business website and made the boss proud; certainly you deserve a raise. You can now go to the live web form and make a submission to check that an email was delivered to the correct department.

This has been a basic example of working with these different services, however, much more can be done in the processing here. For example, if you have existing customers somewhere in a database, the script could pull that information and include it in the email, kick off a workflow from Chapter 8, even send you a text message if this is a really important client.

Charts in Sites

Charts are an important way to convey information to coworkers, stakeholders, and even the general public. Built into Google Script is a complete chartmaking service that parallels what is available in the Google Spreadsheet service.

In this section we will look at two charts: one generated from stock information and a second from a spreadsheet. The script will be done as a standalone service so it can be available in the browser as a single page or inserted in your Google Site as a Gadget.

FinanceApp Chart

Maybe you work for a company that has a public stock and you want to display it on your page or maybe you're a trader that needs to quickly display historical stock data from your phone; in any case, Google Script lets you get that data and dress it up in a nice graphical chart.

Pop open a new script, create a file, and name it **Finance**. This will hold the code for retrieving the information from the Finance service and building a data table used by the charts service to make a graphic.

For purpose of example, this function will return the past year of weekly quotes given a stock symbol.

The end date is today, `new Date()`, so when your page is loaded two months from now it is updated to the latest information with no effort on your part. Getting the start date takes a few more methods to tease out but it is exactly one year before. Just remember the direction, start is not from now until then, rather, that time in the past until now.

The `FinanceApp.getHistoricalStockInfo` will return an array of quote objects given the time frame. In the arguments we specify the symbol, start date, and end date. The last parameter is the interval in days that you would like to sample, "7" meaning every week.

You will need to create a dataTable object from the `Charts` service and add columns for month and price. Note that the type of data must be set for each column.

The quotes array is in the parameter `stockInfo` so we call that into a variable `quotes` to shorten up typing it all out every time. Iterate through the quotes array adding a row to the dataTable for each entry. Arguments in the `addRow` method are in the same order as your columns added to the `dataTable`. The `Utilities.formatDate` with an `MMM` gets us just the month for the quote to save some space on the chart. The second argument in the `addRow` method is the closing price.

Issue `dataTable.build();` and return the `dataTable`.

```
/*
 * Builds the chart dataTable from a stock info
 *
 * Arguments:
 * Name          Type     Description
 * stockSymbol   string   a valid stock symbol ie goog
 *
 * returns DataTable()
 */
function buildFromFinance(stockSymbol) {

  var endDate = new Date();
  var startDate = new Date(new Date(endDate).setFullYear(endDate.getFullYear()-1));
  var stockHist = FinanceApp.getHistoricalStockInfo(stockSymbol, startDate, endDate,
7);

  var dataTable = Charts.newDataTable();
  dataTable.addColumn(Charts.ColumnType.STRING, 'Month');
  dataTable.addColumn(Charts.ColumnType.NUMBER, 'Price');

  var quotes = stockHist.stockInfo;
  for (var i in stockHist.stockInfo)

    dataTable.addRow([Utilities.formatDate(new Date(stockHist.stockInfo[i].time),
"EST", "MMM"),
```

```
                    stockHist.stockInfo[i].close]);
      dataTable.build();
      return dataTable;
}
```

Now that we have a dataTable loaded with a year of stock quotes, we just need to plug the table into a chart.

Go to the Code file and start the standalone UI function.

The first variable is the symbol, which we make static here, but if you want to jazz things up, add a list box or other way for the user to choose a certain quote. Next the dataTable is built using the function you created before. There are several set parameters to allow you customization of the chart, but the most important is plugging in the data using the setDataTable method and issuing the build command.

```
function doGet() {

    var app = UiApp.createApplication().setTitle("Stock Chart");
    var symbol = 'goog';
    var data = buildFromFinance(symbol);

    var chart = Charts.newLineChart()
        .setDimensions(600, 300)
        .setDataTable(data)
        .setColors(['#006400'])
        .setBackgroundColor('transparent')
        .setCurveStyle(Charts.CurveStyle.SMOOTH)
        .setTitle('Last 12 Months for '+symbol.toUpperCase())
        .build();

    var title = app.createLabel('Custom Stock Quotes');

    //Style goes here

    app.add(chart);
    app.add(title);

    return app;
}
```

Add the chart and title to the app and you are ready to publish the page. Figure 9-4 shows the published page loaded in a new browser window. It looks good, but we can make it better with the power of CSS.

Open a new file, and name it CSS. You will need a function to apply the CSS and three objects holding the style attributes.

```
function applyCSS_(element, style){
    for (var key in style){
        element.setStyleAttribute(key, style[key]);
    }
}
```

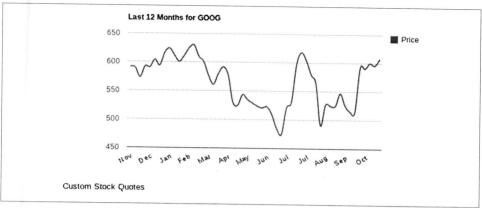

Figure 9-4. You can put these in an email as well

```
var _background =
    {
    "position":"fixed",
    "top":"0px",
    "left":"0px"
    }

var _chart =
    {
    "position":"fixed",
    "top":"0px",
    "left":"0px"
    }

var _title =
    {
    "position":"fixed",
    "top":"265px",
    "left":"30px",
    "color":"#0000FF",
    "font-size":"24",
    "font-family":"cursive,Times New Roman"
    }
```

Using the `"position":"fixed"` parameter frees widgets from inlining and allows you to stack them on top of each other.

The order that widgets stack is determined by when they are added on the page. The first thing added is at the bottom.

Go back to the Code file and add the formatting at the place marker. Choose an image for the background and load it on the app as the bottom item. Apply the CSS to the widgets, save, and reload the published page. See Figure 9-5.

```
    var background = app.createImage('https://5079980847011989849-a-'
        +'1802744773732722657-s-sites.googlegroups.com/site/scriptsexamples/WallSt
%281%29.png');
    background.setSize('600px', '300px');
    app.add(background);
    applyCSS_(background, _background);
    applyCSS_(title, _title);
    applyCSS_(chart, _chart);
```

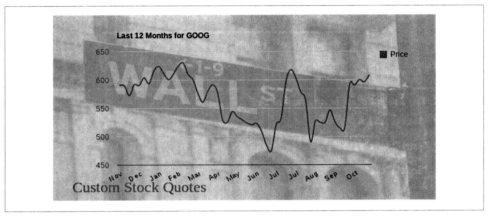

Figure 9-5. CSS makes an OK chart dazzle

Chart from a Spreadsheet

Wouldn't it be great to have a spreadsheet with all your data that automatically generate charts on your Google Site? If that sort of thing is for you, read on, this section will show you how amazingly easy it is to write a script that can be used on most any spreadsheet you want to generate a chart.

The first thing you need is some data and a spreadsheet. In your spreadsheet make the normal header section in row 1 to identify each column. In row 2, you will need a special section to identify what kind of value that column contains: string, number, etc. (See Figure 9-6.)

As in the Finance chart in the last section, a function will be used to create the data table.

In the Code file add the function buildFromSpreadsheet, which takes an argument that is a range of spreadsheet values created by the getValues method from SpreadsheetApp.

Create a data table object and then start iterating the values in range[0], which is row 1 where the headers are. These values are added to the data table as columns. range[1] is the column types and used in the first argument of .addColumn to set the column type.

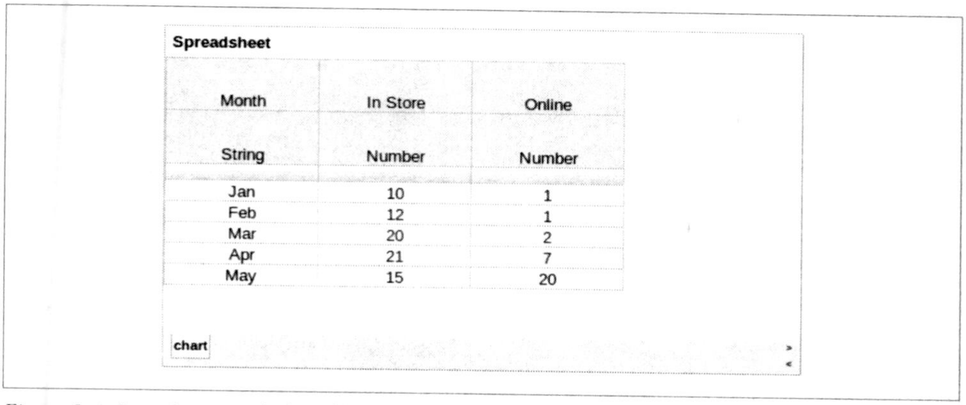

Spreadsheet

Month	In Store	Online
String	Number	Number
Jan	10	1
Feb	12	1
Mar	20	2
Apr	21	7
May	15	20

chart

Figure 9-6. Row 2 can easily be added to spreadsheets feed by a form

The next for loop starts on row 3, in the array index 2, and adds each row. The argument for addRow is comma separated by column values, which is how each row is formatted in range[i].

Build the data table and return it. That is all there is to building the data table.

```
function buildFromSpreadsheet(range){
    var dataTable = Charts.newDataTable();

    for (var j in range[0]) //create the columns
        dataTable.addColumn(Charts.ColumnType[range[1][j].toUpperCase()], range[0][j]);

    for (var i=2; i< range.length; i++) //create the rows
        dataTable.addRow(range[i]);

    dataTable.build();

    return dataTable;
}
```

To use this new function, you will get the data range as values from the spreadsheet. For this example, use getDataRange but you can also use any of the other range calls as long as the first two rows match the header column type scheme.

After buildFromSpreadsheet returns your data table you are ready to build the chart object. This one is an Area Chart and has only a few settings to consider. Setting the range will help the readability and the title will tell the user what it is.

```
function doGet() {

    var range = SpreadsheetApp.openById('<YOUR Spreadsheet ID>')
                .getSheetByName('chart').getDataRange().getValues();

    var data = buildFromSpreadsheet(range);

    var chart = Charts.newAreaChart()
        .setDataTable(data)
```

```
        .setStacked()
        .setRange(0, 40)
        .setTitle("Sales per Month")
        .build();

    var app = UiApp.createApplication().setTitle("My Chart");
    app.add(chart);

    return uiApp;
}
```

Create a UiApp instance and add the chart. Publish the script and load up the page. Figure 9-7 shows the final product. A simple non-CSS version like this can work very well in-line on a Google Sites page.

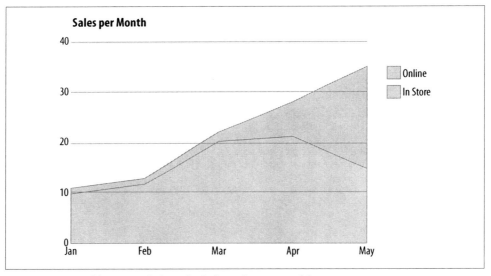

Figure 9-7. Try adding several charts built from the one set of data

City, State—List Box Duo

If you have ever filled out a web form, and I know you have, then it likely asked you for information that is displayed depending on a choice you have made. In this section, we are going to look at the interaction of two list boxes where you select a state and then will be given a choice of several cities.

Start off creating an new UI and publish the script.

A grid will be used to hold the two list boxes and the results from the user's selections.

```
function doGet(e) {
    var app = UiApp.createApplication()
```

```
var grid = app.createGrid(3,2).setCellPadding(10);
app.add(grid);

grid.setText(0, 0, 'State');
grid.setText(1, 0, 'City');
grid.setText(2, 0, 'Result:');

return app;
}
```

Now add two list boxes with the choices for the state.

 If you plan on using a city/state combination like this, it would be a good idea to pull the information from a web service or create a spreadsheet with the choices.

For this example the values will be added using the addItem method. When a user makes a selection the changeList2 function will run:

```
//The State list
var list1 = app.createListBox().setId('list1').setName('list1');
grid.setWidget(0, 1, list1).setId('grid');

list1.addItem('Select');
list1.addItem('NM');
list1.addItem('OR');


var handler = app.createServerChangeHandler('changeList2');
handler.addCallbackElement(grid);
list1.addChangeHandler(handler);
```

In the changeList2 function, use e.parameter.list1 to get the value of the State list box. Because a choice has been made, you want to update the UI and show a list box containing the cities for the given State.

Create a list box for the cities and add a **Select** choice, which will show as the first choice. Now add a handler to manage user selections and run the results function.

```
function changeList2(e){

  var app = UiApp.getActiveApplication();

  var list1Value = e.parameter.list1 //this is the name from list1

   //the City list
  var list2 = app.createListBox().setId('list2').setName('list2');
  app.getElementById('grid').setWidget(1, 1, list2);

  list2.addItem('Select');

  var handler2 = app.createServerChangeHandler('results');
```

```
handler2.addCallbackElement(app.getElementById('grid'));
list2.addChangeHandler(handler2);
```

Because the choices a user can make are limited to what is in `list1`, a JavaScript switch can be used to fill `list2` with the correct information. Again, you will likely want to load this information into a database of some kind and parse it to add the values to the list box. The `NM` case shows how that can be done if the information comes in as an array like the values returned from a spreadsheet range.

```
switch (list1Value){

  case 'OR':
    list2.addItem('Ashland');
    list2.addItem('Portland');
    list2.addItem('Bandon');
    break;

  case 'NM':
    //Here loading from an array is shown
    var cities = ['Albuquerque','Las Cruces','Santa Fe'];
    for(i in cities){
      list2.addItem(cities[i]);
    }
}
return app;
}
```

When the user loaded the UI, it had the state choice, then they made a selection and a city box appeared on the page with the correct information. In most cases the city box would not have a handler and you would continue down the form. However, to shorten the code in this example a handler was attached to the city list and will run the `results` function to show how the values from both list boxes could be used in your script.

Because both list boxes have names and the callback element is the grid, you simply call `e.parameter<listNumber>` to get the values.

```
function results(e){
  var app = UiApp.getActiveApplication();

  app.getElementById('grid').setText(2, 1, e.parameter.list2 + ', ' +
e.parameter.list1);

  return app;
}
```

Figure 9-8 shows the completed product after making both choices.

Figure 9-8. *Context sensitive list boxes are very common in UIs*

Get Social with Google APIs

The core of this section will show you the Google API console where dozens of APIs can be accessed and set up. Because they all work very similar to each other, knowing one should get you most of the way there on the others.

Start by going to Google APIs Console (*https://code.google.com/apis/console/*). In the console you manage your API access by making projects.

> The APIs Console gives you a way to manage your projects that require access using APIs and shows usage and quotas. You can also pay to increase limits and store data.

Under the Google APIs logo there is a list box where you can select "Create." Figure 9-9 shows naming your new API project.

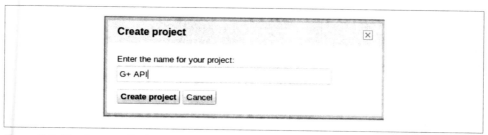

Figure 9-9. *Naming your Project*

Once you have created a new project you will need to enable the APIs that you would like to access, as shown in Figure 9-10. For this example the only API needed is the Google+ API; click the off switch to turn it on. Note that your app will only be able to make 1,000 calls per day to G+.

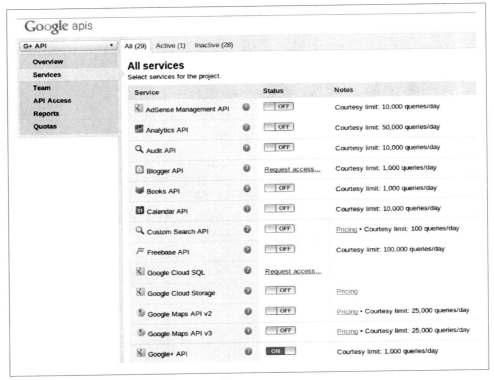

Figure 9-10. Each project can access many APIs

Now that you have enabled the service, you need to get the key from the API Access window shown in Figure 9-11. Your service is web-based, allowing you to use the simple API Access option. There are more options to limit access and such, but for now simply copy the API key.

Every Google API has a document page to help you work with the service using JSON, which is what we will use from our script with the UrlFetch service. Go over to the Google+ API documentation (*http://developers.google.com/+/api/*) and look down the page for API Calls. This section tells us that to access a certain person on Google+, you need to send a request to `https://www.googleapis.com/plus/v1/people/{userId}`. No problem there, all you need to do is visit someone's profile and copy the long number from the URL but if you try a `get` with only this information you will get an error.

The secret is adding your API key so that Google can track your quota. After the `userId` append `?alt=json&key=<Your_Key>`.

Below is a function that takes the argument of a Google+ ID and returns a JavaScript object with the profile's information:

```
function byUserId(gPlusId){
```

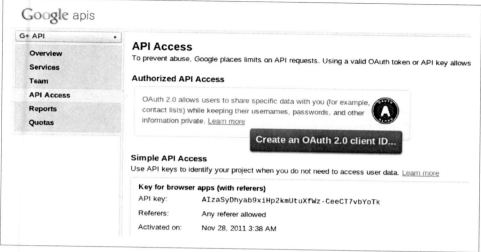

Figure 9-11. Each project has a key

```
var result = UrlFetchApp.fetch("https://www.googleapis.com/plus/v1/people/"+gPlusId+
                    "?alt=json&key=AIzaSyDhyab9xiHp2kmUtuXfWz-CeeCT7vbYoTk");
var plusObject = Utilities.jsonParse(result.getContentText());

return plusObject;
}
```

That really was the tricky part, now you need a UI to display the user's profile. Create a new UI and publish it then make an array with the IDs of the people you want to display in your application. Because you are calling the function byUserId in the array, each element in the array will be created as an object containing all the information that was sent back from the request.

```
function doGet(){

    var plusPeople = [byUserId('114722221595593597247'),
byUserId('109060419131235223303')];

    var app = UiApp.createApplication().setTitle("Google Plus API");
```

This example will display the Google+ profile name, their profile picture, and a link that goes to their profile. Because it uses an array of G+ IDs and can display many profiles on a page, a Flex Table will be used to hold each profile.

Iterate the plusPeople array. A (1,2) grid is used to give the effect of the person's picture next to their name.

Add each of the profile grids to the table.

```
    var table = app.createFlexTable();
    app.add(table);

    for (var i in plusPeople){
```

```
        var grid = app.createGrid(1,2);
        table.setWidget(parseInt(i), 0, grid);
        grid.setWidget(0, 0,
  app.createImage(plusPeople[i].image.url).setSize('100px','100px'));

        var infoTable = app .createFlexTable();
        grid.setWidget(0, 1, infoTable);

        infoTable.setWidget(0, 0, app.createAnchor(plusPeople[i].displayName,
  plusPeople[i].url)
                          .setStyleAttribute("font-size", "28px"));

    }
```

Figure 9-12 shows the finished application. To recap, many of Google's APIs have moved to the new API console, which requires a few extra steps to set up, but also gives you better control over the access without having to build it into your application.

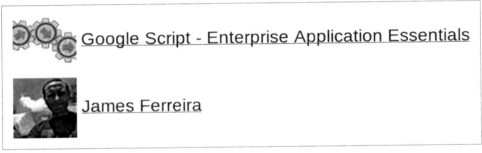

Figure 9-12. G+ People, listed

Progress Indicators

In our twitchy culture, everything must happen instantly or the world may very well end. However, as reality sets in, some things may take a while to complete and your applications should be able to indicate that. For example, your application may need to calculate values from all over the Web and you can't count on other sites to perform as well as your carefully planned code. The problem is that if the user does not see some kind of acknowledgement that they have conveyed their intent for your application to do something, they may think you don't care or that your application is broken. Therefore, if you know that the processing will take some time to complete, give the user something to keep them entertained while they wait.

The UiApp must return to update the page with new information; this means that you can't display anything until it gets done doing what you asked, one click per action. Normally we would use a click handler to perform a task on a button press, but that only has a single action behavior and we need to run two functions. One function to display the progress indicator and a second to perform the task. You could wire up two click handlers to one button, both with their own functions but it is completely unstable, and for odd reasons one or the other handlers may not fire every time.

Client side handlers are a new feature of Google Script that makes adding progress indicators very easy. When the button is pressed, a client side handler runs on the user's computer without needing to go all the way to Mountain View to do something like change the visibility of an element.

 Client side handlers get along great with server handlers. You can also add several client side targets to the same handler, showing some things while hiding others completely—possible in just one click.

The concept will be to put a progress indicator image on the page but set its visibility to false so it is hidden. We will use an animated gif of a spinning thing like you see on most every computer while it processes. When the button is pressed the client handler shows the image and a server handler performs the work. When the server handler returns, it hides the image again.

Start a new script and publish it. This example is meant to show you how to add progress indicators to your own apps and will focus only on the parts required to add this functionality. There will be a few labels added to the app indicating what one should do, but these are to be removed when you plug this script into your own.

Build a grid to hold the different parts of the indicator. Only the animated spinner or a line of text is needed to give the feedback. Both are used here to show how they work together. A third label is used to indicate when the process is done.

```
function doGet() {
  var app = UiApp.createApplication().setTitle('Spinners');

  app.add(app.createLabel('After clicking the button below a progress indicator'));
  app.add(app.createLabel('will simulate a long load time'));

  //A simple button
  var button = app.createButton('Load');

  //use the url of an animated gif
  var spinner = app.createImage('https://5079980847011989849-a-1802744773732722657'+
                                '-s-sites.googlegroups.com/site/scriptsexamples/
ProgressSpinner.gif')
                                .setVisible(false)
                                .setId('spinner');
  var spinLabel = app.createLabel('Please wait while I figure this out')
                                .setVisible(false)
                                .setId('spinLabel');
  var doneLabel = app.createLabel('All done, thank you for waiting')
                                .setVisible(false)
                                .setId('doneLabel');

  var grid = app.createGrid(5,1).setId('grid');
```

```
    app.add(grid);
    grid.setWidget(1, 0, button);
    grid.setWidget(2,0, spinner);
    grid.setWidget(3,0, spinLabel);
    grid.setWidget(4,0, doneLabel);

//Client Handler

//Server handler

    return app;
}
```

Next add a Client Handler to show the spinner and spinLabel elements. You get them using the forTargets method and setting their visible property to true. Add a second forTargets method to set the doneLabel to false. This way if the user presses the button again, the doneLabel will vanish.

```
var loadSpinner = app.createClientHandler()
            .forTargets(spinner,spinLabel)
              .setVisible(true)
            .forTargets(doneLabel)
              .setVisible(false);
button.addClickHandler(loadSpinner);
```

The next part is to add a Server Handler. This is the handler you would normally use to perform the work. Make sure to pass the grid directly or as a child element in the callback.

```
var load = app.createServerHandler('loadImages')
            .addCallbackElement(grid);
button.addClickHandler(load);
```

The loadImages() function is what runs when you press the button. It does not really do anything in our example except to cause the script to sleep for five seconds, simulating a long calculation is taking place.

 The maximum amount of time a script can run on the server is five minutes before it times out.

After the time is up, we hide the spinner and spinLabel elements and show the doneLabel before returning the function:

```
function loadImages(){
  var app = UiApp.getActiveApplication();
  //simulated load time
  Utilities.sleep(5000); //5 seconds
  //You would replace this sleep timer with whatever process you have.

  //At the end hide the image
  app.getElementById('spinner').setVisible(false);
  app.getElementById('spinLabel').setVisible(false);
```

```
    app.getElementById('doneLabel').setVisible(true);

    return app;
}
```

Figure 9-13 shows the application just after pressing the button. Of course your application will look much better on the screen with the animation.

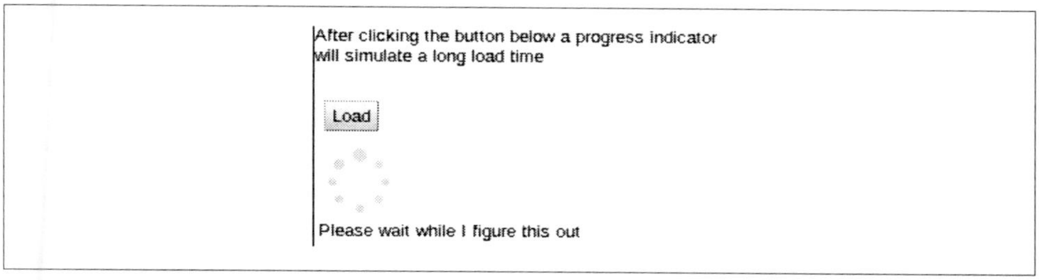

Figure 9-13. Progress entertainment

PART III

UI Element Examples

There are a lot of widgets in the UiApp and this part of the book is devoted to giving you examples of how each one works. While these are working examples to get you started, you will want to refer to the documentation on the Google Script site for the full details.

UI Element Examples

Boxes

Check Box

The check box: who knows where they came from, but how could we possibly live without them? A check box is a yes/no type of element that stands on its own, unlike radio buttons, which look similar but only allow a single selection. You can have 1 or 100 check boxes on a page and each has its own value.

In this example, you will check a box and click Submit. Typically you would have several elements on a page along with check boxes, and you will need to read if the box is checked along with other information.

Reference: *http://code.google.com/googleapps/appsscript/class_checkbox.html*

```
function checkBox(){
  var mydoc = SpreadsheetApp.getActiveSpreadsheet();
  var app = UiApp.createApplication().setTitle('Check Box Example');

//A button to take care of the submission.
  var mybutton = app.createButton('Submit');
//using setName will give you the ability to get the value
  var myCheckBox = app.createCheckBox().setName('myCheckBox');
//A label will be used to give feedback on the value of the checkBox
  var infoLabel = app.createLabel('Check the box and click submit').setId('infoLabel');

//the next 3 lines add a handler to preform a function when the submit button is
clicked
  var handler = app.createServerClickHandler('changeMe_');
  handler.addCallbackElement(myCheckBox);
  mybutton.addClickHandler(handler);

//put everything in the UI
  app.add(myCheckBox);
  app.add(mybutton);
  app.add(infoLabel);
```

```
    mydoc.show(app);
}

function changeMe_(e){
    var app = UiApp.getActiveApplication();
    app.getElementById('infoLabel').setText('Check box is: ' + e.parameter.myCheckBox);
    return app;
}
```

List Box

The list box is your tool of choice if a user will need to select an item from a long list of options. Not only that, but it is a great way to save space and give your user a way of seeing without question what they have selected. There are two ways to work a listBox: on select and as a value passed through a handler. On select will immediately fire a handler once the user makes a choice. For example, you may present more options to appear or send the user to a different panel. The static choice will leave the selection as the selected value and close the list. You would use this when your user is performing other interactions and then passing all the values through a handler. Think of a form with many selections, or see Figure A-1.

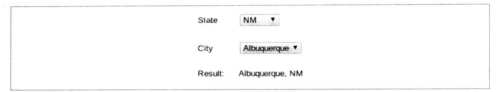

Figure A-1. A pair of list boxes

This example includes an onChange handler so you can see how an on select scenario plays out.

Reference: *http://www.google.com/google-d-s/scripts/class_listbox.html*

```
function doGet(e) {
  var app = UiApp.createApplication();

//using setName will give you the ability to get the value
  var dropDownList = app.createListBox().setName('list');

//A label will be used to demonstrate the optional onChange function
  var infoLabel = app.createLabel('click to change').setId('infoLabel');

//addItem fills the list
  dropDownList.addItem("one");
  dropDownList.addItem("two");
  dropDownList.addItem("three");

//the next 3 optional lines add a handler to preform a function when a choice is
```

```
made
  var handler = app.createServerClickHandler('changeMe');
  handler.addCallbackElement(dropDownList);
  dropDownList.addChangeHandler(handler);

  app.add(dropDownList);
  app.add(infoLabel);
  return app;
}

//This is the optional onChange function
function changeMe(e){
  var app = UiApp.getActiveApplication();
  app.getElementById('infoLabel').setText('You chose: ' + e.parameter.list);
  return app;
}
```

Password Box

Password boxes are passwords the easy way. This widget is basically a text box (See Figure A-2), but it hides the characters as you type to prevent eavesdropping. It will also allow setting a text value if you would like to use a "remember password" setup. You will need to do your own encryption because the output is a string in clear text.

Reference: *http://code.google.com/googleapps/appsscript/class_passwordtextbox.html*

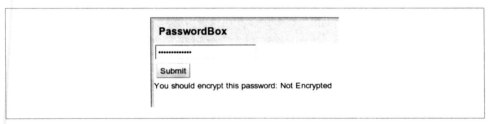

Figure A-2. Password box example

```
function PasswordBox() {
  var mydoc = SpreadsheetApp.getActiveSpreadsheet();
  var app = UiApp.createApplication().setTitle('PasswordBox');

  //a vertical panel to hold the widgets
  var vPanel = app.createVerticalPanel().setId('vPanel');
  app.add(vPanel);

  //Create the password box
  var pwBox = app.createPasswordTextBox().setName('pwBox');
  vPanel.add(pwBox);

  //A button to click
  var button = app.createButton('Submit').setId('button');
  vPanel.add(button);
```

```
    //This label will return our password
    var label = app.createLabel('').setId('label');
    vPanel.add(label);

    //A button handler
    var handler = app.createServerClickHandler('getPw_');
    handler.addCallbackElement(vPanel);
    button.addClickHandler(handler);

    mydoc.show(app);
}

function getPw_(e){
    var app = UiApp.getActiveApplication();
    //we will simply return the entered password in clear text
    app.getElementById('label').setText('You should encrypt this password: ' +
e.parameter.pwBox);
    return app;
}
```

Buttons

There are many kinds of buttons you can add to a UI and they all share the same basic elements (see Figure A-3):

- Button widget
- Handler
- Function to call

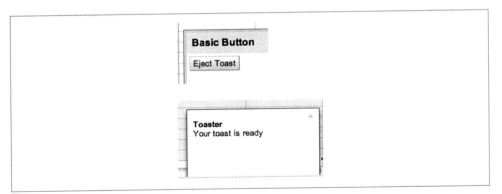

Figure A-3. The basic button

The basic button code:

```
function BasicButton() {
    var mydoc = SpreadsheetApp.getActiveSpreadsheet();
    var app = UiApp.createApplication().setTitle('Basic Button');
    var mainPanel = app.createVerticalPanel().setId('mainPanel');
```

```
    app.add(mainPanel);

    //create a button and add to the panel
    var button = app.createButton('Eject Toast');
    mainPanel.add(button);

    //create a handler for the button that calls the function toaster
    var handler = app.createServerClickHandler('toaster');
    //In order to access elements you must assign a callback
    //all child elements are available to the fuction you are passing for the parent
    handler.addCallbackElement(mainPanel);
    //add the handler to the button
    button.addClickHandler(handler);

    mydoc.show(app);
}


function toaster() {
    var ss = SpreadsheetApp.getActiveSpreadsheet();
    ss.toast('Your toast is ready', 'Toaster');
}
```

Push Button

The push button (see Figure A-4) is a regular button with a few extra tricks, most notably it can have two arguments for the text string `app.createPushButton('Press', 'Hold')`. The first is displayed when the button is not doing anything, the second shows when the button is pushed and held. The example will demonstrate the push button function by displaying the time when the button is pressed down and again when it is released.

Reference: *http://code.google.com/googleapps/appsscript/class_pushbutton.html*

Figure A-4. Push button

```
    function PushButton() {
        var mydoc = SpreadsheetApp.getActiveSpreadsheet();
        var app = UiApp.createApplication().setTitle('Push Button');
        var vPanel = app.createVerticalPanel().setId('vPanel');
        app.add(vPanel);

        //Note that a pushButton has more than one argument
        var pushButton = app.createPushButton('Press', 'Hold');
```

```
pushButton.setWidth('100px').setStyleAttribute('text-align', 'center');
vPanel.add(pushButton);

//Two labels to show button pressing times
var label = app.createLabel().setId('label');
vPanel.add(label);

var label2 = app.createLabel().setId('label2');
vPanel.add(label2);

//Two handlers, one for mouse down the other up
var handler1 = app.createServerMouseHandler('startPress_');
handler1.addCallbackElement(vPanel);
pushButton.addMouseDownHandler(handler1);

var handler2 = app.createServerMouseHandler('endPress_');
handler2.addCallbackElement(vPanel);
pushButton.addMouseUpHandler(handler2);

mydoc.show(app);
}

function startPress_(e){
  var app = UiApp.getActiveApplication();
  var startTime = new Date();
  //some date formating
  startTime = Utilities.formatDate(startTime, 'GMT', 'HH:mm:ss')
  //add the date to the label
  app.getElementById('label').setText('Button Pressed at: ' + startTime.toString());

  return app;
}

function endPress_(e){
  var app = UiApp.getActiveApplication();
  var endTime = new Date();
  endTime = Utilities.formatDate(endTime, 'GMT', 'HH:mm:ss')
  app.getElementById('label2').setText('Button Released at: ' + endTime.toString());

  return app;
}
```

Radio Button

Radio buttons, shown in Figure A-5, are used when you have several choices but only one can be true; think all those multiple choice tests you took on scantron. On the Web we have a bit more control than the #2 pencil and eraser. Each time a user clicks a radio, that radio is set true and a dot shows in the center, any previously set radio in the group is deselected, thus the user can choose only one. A practical example would be on a form where you are asking the sex of the applicant by providing "Male" and "Female" choices.

Figure A-5. Radio buttons

Radio buttons use the form panel to function correctly. If you need them to operate outside of a form, they are not managed as a group.

Reference: *http://code.google.com/googleapps/appsscript/class_radiobutton.html*

```
function RadioButtons() {
  var mydoc = SpreadsheetApp.getActiveSpreadsheet();
  var app = UiApp.createApplication().setTitle('Radio Buttons');

//to use radios you will need a form
  var form = app.createFormPanel().setId('form').setEncoding('multipart/form-data');

//make a few radio buttons
//each radios that are choices go in a group
  var myRadio1 = app.createRadioButton("radio", "one").setFormValue('one');
  var myRadio2 = app.createRadioButton("radio", "two").setFormValue('two');
  var myRadio3 = app.createRadioButton("radio", "three").setFormValue('three');

//create a form and put the radios in it
  var formContent = app.createGrid().resize(4,1);
    form.add(formContent);

    formContent.setWidget(0, 0, myRadio1);
    formContent.setWidget(1, 0, myRadio2);
    formContent.setWidget(2, 0, myRadio3);
    formContent.setWidget(3, 0, app.createSubmitButton('Submit!'));

  app.add(form);
//a label will be used to display the value sent to the handler
  app.add(app.createLabel('').setVisible(false).setId('info'));

  mydoc.show(app);
}

function doPost(e) {
  var app = UiApp.getActiveApplication();
//use the group name to get the value of the selected radio
  var radio = e.parameter.radio;
  app.getElementById('info').setVisible(true).setText('You selected ' + radio);
  return app;
}
```

Reset Button

It is terribly inconvenient to delete a bunch of text boxes; lucky for us the UiApp gives us the Reset Button, shown in Figure A-6. This button must be a child of the form panel to work and does not require a handler, making it a snap to use.

 Reset buttons only work with form panels.

Reference: *http://code.google.com/googleapps/appsscript/class_resetbutton.html*

Reset Button	
Type something	this will be reset,
	Reset

Figure A-6. Reset button

```
function ResetButton() {
    var mydoc = SpreadsheetApp.getActiveSpreadsheet();
    var app = UiApp.createApplication().setTitle('Reset Button');

    //create the form panel
    var form = app.createFormPanel().setId('frm').setEncoding('multipart/form-data');
    app.add(form);

    //Make a grid
    var formContent = app.createGrid().resize(2,2);
    form.add(formContent);

    //Add content to the grid
    formContent.setText(0, 0, 'Type something')
    formContent.setWidget(0, 1, app.createTextBox().setName('fileName'));
    formContent.setWidget(1, 1, app.createResetButton('Reset'));

    mydoc.show(app);
}
```

Toggle Button

The Toggle Button, as shown in Figure A-7, is not something you see very often anymore. The idea of the mechanical button was that you press it and it stays down, press again and it pops back up. Our digital version is the same. Give it a click and it visually changes to appear that it is down, push again and it goes back to the original look. An additional feature is that the up and down states can change the text of the button.

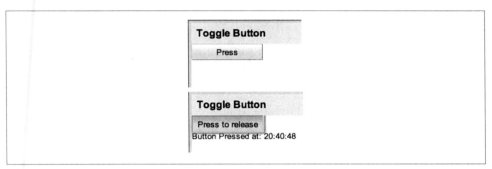

Figure A-7. Toggle button

Reference: *http://code.google.com/googleapps/appsscript/class_togglebutton.html*

```
function ToggleButton() {
  var mydoc = SpreadsheetApp.getActiveSpreadsheet();
  var app = UiApp.createApplication().setTitle('Toggle Button');
  var vPanel = app.createVerticalPanel().setId('vPanel');
  app.add(vPanel);

  //Note that a taggle button has more than one argument
  var toggleButton = app.createToggleButton('Press', 'Press to
release').setId('toggleButton');
  toggleButton.setWidth('100px').setStyleAttribute('text-align', 'center');
  vPanel.add(toggleButton);

  //Two labels to show button pressing times
  var label = app.createLabel().setId('label');
  vPanel.add(label);

  //Two handlers, one for mouse down the other up
  var handler1 = app.createServerMouseHandler('buttonPress_');
  handler1.addCallbackElement(vPanel);
  toggleButton.addMouseDownHandler(handler1);

  mydoc.show(app);
}

function buttonPress_(e){
  var app = UiApp.getActiveApplication();
  var startTime = new Date();
  //some date formating
  startTime = Utilities.formatDate(startTime, 'GMT', 'HH:mm:ss')
  //add the date to the label
  app.getElementById('label').setText('Button Pressed at: ' + startTime.toString());

  return app;
}
```

Submit Button

If you see a bunch of text boxes on a web page, it is a sure bet you are looking at a form. While GAS offers many ways to submit information to a function, the Form Panel and Submit button (see Figure A-8) combination can save several lines of code. There are some special tricks here as well. Like the Reset button, the Submit button does not require a handler to do its job. However, this also means you will need to use the doPost(e) function to handle your form. When you add a handler to a normal button only the elements in the callback will be available to you. Submit makes all of the elements in the root panel (UiApp. createApplication()) available in doPost. After do-Post runs, you get the added bonus of the form panel automatically being hidden.

 Requires a form panel and doPost function.

Reference: *http://code.google.com/googleapps/appsscript/class_submitbutton.html*

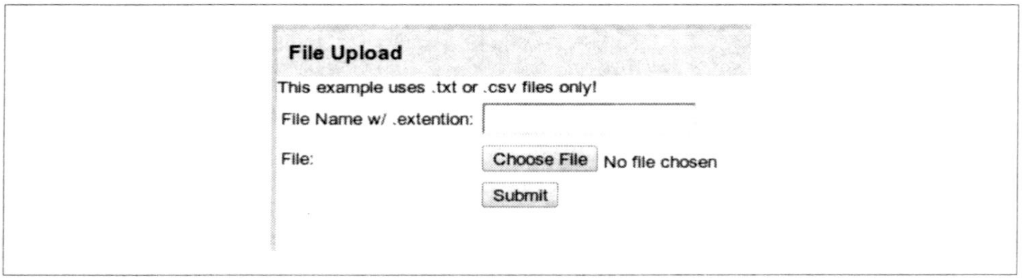

File Upload

This example uses .txt or .csv files only!

File Name w/ .extention:

File: Choose File   No file chosen

Submit

Figure A-8. Submit button

```
function SubmitButton() {
  var mydoc = SpreadsheetApp.getActiveSpreadsheet();
  var app = UiApp.createApplication().setTitle('Submit Button');

  //A label to provide some feedback
  var label = app.createLabel('Type your name and click Submit').setId('label');
  app.add(label);

  //create the form panel
  var form = app.createFormPanel().setId('form').setEncoding('multipart/form-data');
  app.add(form);

  //Make a grid
  var formContent = app.createGrid().resize(2,2);
  form.add(formContent);

  //Add content to the grid
  formContent.setText(0, 0, 'Your Name: ')
  formContent.setWidget(0, 1, app.createTextBox().setName('yourName'));
  formContent.setWidget(1, 1, app.createSubmitButton('Submit'));
```

```
  mydoc.show(app);
}

//The form panel/submit button combo uses doPost
function doPost(e){
  var app = UiApp.getActiveApplication();
  app.getElementById('label').setText('Thank you ' + e.parameter.yourName);
  return app;
}
```

File Upload

Web apps are interactive and sometimes that means getting files from the local computer (yes, some people still keep them there) and upload them. The file chooser gives
you the typical GUI to choose your file from the file system and takes care of all the
path information. It also takes care of creating a button and the label with file information. One thing to watch out for is you will need to handle your own "no file selected"
notification.

 File uploads (see Figure A-9) require a Form Panel, and at the time of
this writing, this feature only works in Google Apps Premier.

Reference: *http://code.google.com/googleapps/appsscript/class_fileupload.html*

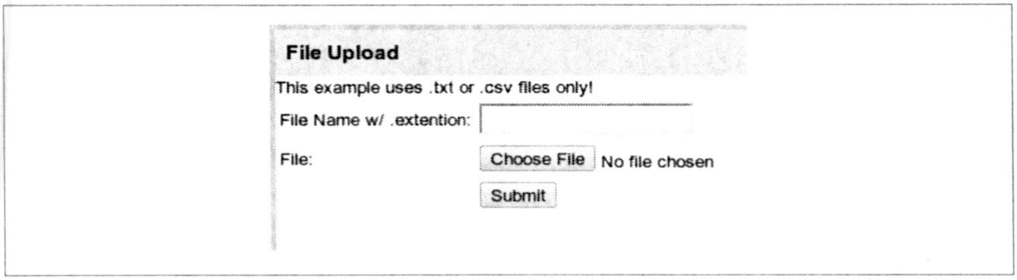

File Upload

This example uses .txt or .csv files only!

File Name w/ .extention: _____

File: [Choose File] No file chosen

                 [Submit]

Figure A-9. File upload

```
function FileUpload() {
  var mydoc = SpreadsheetApp.getActiveSpreadsheet();
  var app = UiApp.createApplication().setTitle('File Upload');

  //A label to provide some feedback
  var label = app.createLabel('This example uses .txt or .csv files
only!').setId('label');
  app.add(label);

  //create the form panel
  var form = app.createFormPanel().setId('form').setEncoding('multipart/form-data');
```

```
    app.add(form);

    //Make a grid
    var formContent = app.createGrid().resize(3,2);
    form.add(formContent);

    //Add content to the grid
    formContent.setText(0, 0, 'File Name w/ .extention: ')
    formContent.setWidget(0, 1, app.createTextBox().setName('fileName'));
    formContent.setWidget(1, 0, app.createLabel('File:'));
    formContent.setWidget(1, 1, app.createFileUpload());
    formContent.setWidget(2, 1, app.createSubmitButton('Submit'));

    mydoc.show(app);
}

//The form panel/submit button combo uses doPost
function doPost(e){
  var app = UiApp.getActiveApplication();
  var fileName = e.parameter.fileName;
  var yourFile = e.parameter.file;

  DocsList.createFile(fileName, yourFile);

  app.getElementById('label').setText('Look in your Docs list for the file');
  return app;
}
```

Flex Table

Flex Tables (see Figure A-10) are great when you don't know how many rows or columns you might need. You simply set the content in a cell and the table will automatically adjust. A Flex Table can take both text and widgets, making it versatile. Often one may be getting a certain set of information from a spreadsheet or database. Because you don't know how many records that will contain, a grid will simply not work.

Adding values to a Flex Table come in two varieties: flexTable.setText(0, 0, 'text String'); and flexTable.setWidget(0, 0, widget);. Inside the parentheses are the cell locations and a value. Flex Tables are zero-based so (0, 0) is the upper-left cell. Keep in mind that the first number is the row and the second number is the column. The next argument is the value of the cell: (row, column, value). The example below will show how flexible the Flex Table is by automatically adjusting to the values you feed it from an array.

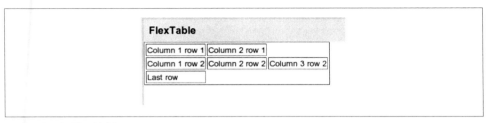

Figure A-10. Flex Table

```
function FlexTable() {
  var mydoc = SpreadsheetApp.getActiveSpreadsheet();
  var app = UiApp.createApplication().setTitle('FlexTable');

  //this is a 2D array[][]
  //when you .getValues() from a spreadsheet you get a 2D array
  var array2D = [["Column 1 row 1", "Column 2 row 1"],
                 ["Column 1 row 2", "Column 2 row 2", "Column 3 row 2"],
                 ["Last row"]];

  var verticalPanel = app.createVerticalPanel();
  app.add(verticalPanel);

  var flexTable = app.createFlexTable();
  verticalPanel.add(flexTable);

  //a bit of style to make the table easy to read
  flexTable.setBorderWidth(1);

  //here is where the flextable shines
  //you can give it as many values as you like
  for (i in array2D){
    for (j in array2D[i]){
      flexTable.setText(parseInt(i), parseInt(j), array2D[i][j]);
    }
  }
  mydoc.show(app);
}
```

Grid

This book is about building web apps and to give the user a familiar web page look, we will need the help of a few grids. The grid is to GAS what tables are to HTML but much simpler to code. Start by creating a grid and setting how many rows and columns it will have (app.createGrid(rows, columns)). Then you simply add elements: grid.set Widget(row, column, yourWidget).

Be careful! Grids are zero-based so while you may create a (3, 3) grid, setWidget(3, 3, widget) will error because the grid range started at (0, 0) thus (2, 2,) is the top.

Table A-1. Layout of cell locations in a zero-based grid widget

0,0	0,1	0,2
1,0	1,1	1,1
2,0	2,1	2,2

In this example, you build a simple web page layout. There will be two grids, one within the other, to give the look of a full width banner and a three column content section. See Figure A-11.

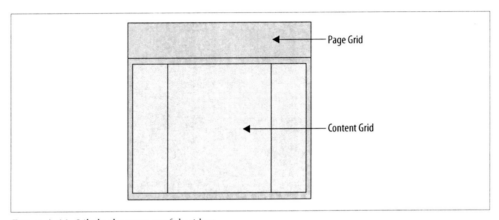

Figure A-11. Likely the most useful widget

With the grid, it is easy to build a web page style layout or even a whole Google Script generated website.

Below is the example code to build the layout you see in Figure A-12.

```
function GridExample() {
  var mydoc = SpreadsheetApp.getActiveSpreadsheet();
  var app = UiApp.createApplication().setTitle('Grid
Example').setWidth(473).setHeight(300);
  var mainPanel = app.createVerticalPanel().setId('mainPanel');
  app.add(mainPanel);

  //create a grid 2 cells tall and 1 cell wide
  var grid = app.createGrid(2, 1).setWidth('473px');
  mainPanel.add(grid);

  //add a banner
  grid.setWidget(0, 0, app.createImage('https://docs.google.com/drawings/pub?'+
          'id=1P52wtN-8Q7iuOtGd7dTcnq9B9FAzW8PsWq-o_uo1FJO&w=473&h=61'));

  //create a grid to hold page content
  var contentGrid = app.createGrid(1, 3).setHeight('200px').setCellPadding(10);
```

```
    grid.setWidget(1, 0, contentGrid);

    //add the page content
    contentGrid.setWidget(0, 0, app.createLabel('left side content').setWidth('50px')
                        .setHeight('100%').setStyleAttribute('background', 'silver'));
    contentGrid.setWidget(0, 1, app.createLabel('Page
body').setWidth('300px').setHeight('100%'));
    contentGrid.setWidget(0, 2, app.createLabel('right side content').setWidth('50px')
                        .setHeight('100%').setStyleAttribute('background',
'WhiteSmoke'));

    mydoc.show(app);
}
```

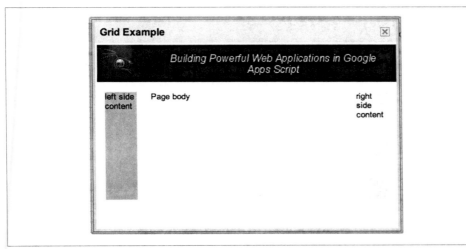

Figure A-12. Very similar to how tables are used in HTML

Hidden

Hidden is just a text box you can't see and does not take up space on the page. See
Figure A-13.

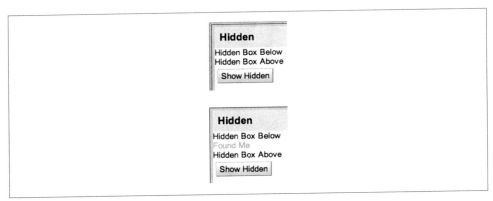

Figure A-13. Now you see me, now you don't.

```
function Hidden() {
  var mydoc = SpreadsheetApp.getActiveSpreadsheet();
  var app = UiApp.createApplication().setTitle('Hidden');
  var mainPanel = app.createVerticalPanel().setId('mainPanel');
  app.add(mainPanel);

  //one label above and one below for reference.
  var label1 = app.createLabel('Hidden Box Below');
  mainPanel.add(label1);

  //This is the hidden box with a value ready to go
  var hiddenBox = app.createHidden().setName('hiddenBox').setValue("Found Me");
  mainPanel.add(hiddenBox);

  //after button press we show a lable to indicate where the box "is"
  var hiddenLabel = app.createLabel().setId('hiddenLabel').setVisible(false);
  mainPanel.add(hiddenLabel);

  var label2 = app.createLabel('Hidden Box Above');
  mainPanel.add(label2);

  //simple button
  var button = app.createButton('Show Hidden');
  mainPanel.add(button);
  var handler = app.createServerClickHandler('getHidden_');
  handler.addCallbackElement(mainPanel);
  button.addClickHandler(handler);

  mydoc.show(app);
}

function getHidden_(e){
  //we passed the mainPanel now we can access its children by name
  var hiddenValue = e.parameter.hiddenBox;
  //create an instance of the active app
  var app = UiApp.getActiveApplication();
  //call on the hiddenLabel to set its value to the hidden box
  app.getElementById('hiddenLabel').setText(hiddenValue)
```

```
                    .setVisible(true)
                    .setStyleAttribute('color', 'orange');

  return app;
}
```

Anchor (Hyperlink)

The Anchor function will allow the insertion of a link into your UI. Most web pages have links to go elsewhere, and this is how you add a link in GS:

```
function Anchor() {
    var mydoc = SpreadsheetApp.getActiveSpreadsheet();
    var app = UiApp.createApplication().setTitle('Anchor');
    var mainPanel = app.createVerticalPanel().setId('mainPanel');
    app.add(mainPanel);

    var googleLink = app.createAnchor('Google', 'http://google.com');
    app.add(googleLink);

    mydoc.show(app);
}
```

Image

In Figure A-14, we add an image. You can set the size and other style attributes like location and even connect a handler. This can give you the opportunity to build very nice button interfaces.

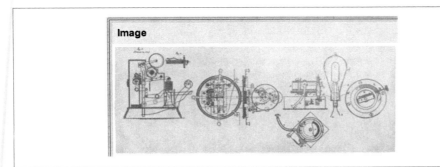

Figure A-14. Images

```
function Image() {
    var mydoc = SpreadsheetApp.getActiveSpreadsheet();
    var app = UiApp.createApplication().setTitle('Image');
    var mainPanel = app.createVerticalPanel().setId('mainPanel');
    app.add(mainPanel);

    var image = app.createImage('http://www.google.com/logos/2011/edison11-hp.gif');
```

```
    mainPanel.add(image);

    mydoc.show(app);
}
```

Label

Labels are used anywhere you need text because at the time of this writing, there is not an HTML widget. Labels have the setStyleAttribute function that will let you apply CSS.

```
function Label() {
    var mydoc = SpreadsheetApp.getActiveSpreadsheet();
    var app = UiApp.createApplication().setTitle('Label');
    var mainPanel = app.createVerticalPanel().setId('mainPanel');
    app.add(mainPanel);

    var label = app.createLabel();
    label.setText('This is a Label');

    mainPanel.add(label);

    mydoc.show(app);
}
```

Text Area

The text area will allow the user to enter several lines of text. This is most well known as the paragraph field. If the text in the box overflows, scroll bars will automatically appear.

```
function TextArea() {
    var mydoc = SpreadsheetApp.getActiveSpreadsheet();
    var app = UiApp.createApplication().setTitle('Text Area');
    var mainPanel = app.createVerticalPanel().setId('mainPanel');
    app.add(mainPanel);

    var ta = app.createTextArea();
    mainPanel.add(ta);

    ta.setSize('300px', '100px');

    mydoc.show(app);
}
```

Text Box

The great text box: every website has at least one, if yours doesn't, don't worry, the browser's address bar is nothing more than a text box so you will never be without. Seriously, most of your user input will be through a text box. The text box is very versatile and can be used on most of the panel widgets. To get a value from a text box you must pass its value through a handler to a function. In the example below we want to also interact with a label so we will add all our elements to a panel and then pass the whole panel. When you pass a widget's value through a handler you can call on that value using dot notation in the parent parameters `e.parameter.textBox`.

If you are getting a value from the text box you need only to name it `.setName('textBox')`. If, however, you need to set a textbox value from the callback, like we do here to clear the value, you will need to also ID the textbox `setId('textBox')`.

As with most widgets, you can set the size and other attributes of the text box; you can even attach a handler to it so that the function runs if the Enter key is pressed.

```
function TextBox() {
    var mydoc = SpreadsheetApp.getActiveSpreadsheet();
    var app = UiApp.createApplication().setTitle('Text Box');

    var mainPanel = app.createVerticalPanel().setId('mainPanel');
    app.add(mainPanel);

    //a lable to give some directions and feedback
    var label = app.createLabel('Please enter your name').setId('label');
    mainPanel.add(label);

    //the text box, you will need setName AND setId
    var textBox = app.createTextBox().setName('textBox').setId('textBox');
    mainPanel.add(textBox);

    //a button to send the text box info to the function addText
    var button = app.createButton('Submit');
    mainPanel.add(button);

    //the button handler
    var handler = app.createServerClickHandler('addText');
    handler.addCallbackElement(mainPanel);
    button.addClickHandler(handler);

    mydoc.show(app);
}

function addText(e){
    var app = UiApp.getActiveApplication();
    //we passed our elements by name when we set the callback as mainPanel
    //to get a value use the dot notation
    var youAre = 'Hello ' + e.parameter.textBox;
    //change the text of the lable
    app.getElementById('label').setText(youAre);
    //clear the textbox
    app.getElementById('textBox').setValue('');
    return app;
}
```

About the Author

James Ferreira managed public communications for two successful state political campaigns; served as the Chief Information Officer for the New Mexico Office of Attorney General; migrated the first government agency to Google Apps; speaks at conferences across the nation about implementing new technology; wrote software to extend Google Apps that serves more than half a million users worldwide and published numerous technology articles including the Google Enterprise blog.

Get even more for your money.

Join the O'Reilly Community, and register the O'Reilly books you own. It's free, and you'll get:

- $4.99 ebook upgrade offer
- 40% upgrade offer on O'Reilly print books
- Membership discounts on books and events
- Free lifetime updates to ebooks and videos
- Multiple ebook formats, DRM FREE
- Participation in the O'Reilly community
- Newsletters
- Account management
- 100% Satisfaction Guarantee

Signing up is easy:

1. **Go to: oreilly.com/go/register**
2. **Create an O'Reilly login.**
3. **Provide your address.**
4. **Register your books.**

Note: English-language books only

To order books online:

oreilly.com/store

For questions about products or an order:

orders@oreilly.com

To sign up to get topic-specific email announcements and/or news about upcoming books, conferences, special offers, and new technologies:

elists@oreilly.com

For technical questions about book content:

booktech@oreilly.com

To submit new book proposals to our editors:

proposals@oreilly.com

O'Reilly books are available in multiple DRM-free ebook formats. For more information:

oreilly.com/ebooks

O'REILLY®

Have it your way.

CPSIA information can be obtained at www.ICGtesting.com
Printed in the USA
BVOW030340091012

302533BV00005B/41/P